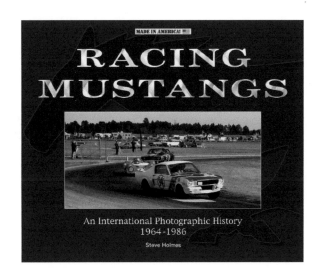

MADE IN AMERICA!

RACING
MUSTANGS

An International Photographic History
1964-1986

Steve Holmes

More great books from Veloce

Essential Buyer's Guide Series
Ford Capri (Paxton)
Ford Escort Mk1 & Mk2 (Williamson)
Ford Focus RS/ST 1st Generation (Williamson)
Ford Model A – All Models 1927 to 1931 (Buckley)
Ford Model T – All models 1909 to 1927 (Barker)
Ford Mustang – First Generation 1964 to 1973 (Cook)
Ford Mustang – Fifth Generation (2005-2014) (Cook)
Ford RS Cosworth Sierra & Escort (Williamson)

Those Were The Days ... Series
Alpine Trials & Rallies 1910-1973 (Pfundner)
Brighton National Speed Trials (Gardiner)
British and European Trucks of the 1970s (Peck)
British Drag Racing – The early years (Pettitt)
British Touring Car Racing (Collins)
Buick Riviera (Mort)
Don Hayter's MGB Story – The birth of the MGB in
 MG's Abingdon Design & Development Office (Hayter)
Endurance Racing at Silverstone in the 1970s & 1980s
 (Parker)
Hot Rod & Stock Car Racing in Britain in the 1980s
 (Neil)
Motor Racing at Brands Hatch in the Seventies (Parker)
Motor Racing at Brands Hatch in the Eighties (Parker)
Motor Racing at Crystal Palace (Collins)
Motor Racing at Goodwood in the Sixties (Gardiner)
Motor Racing at Nassau in the 1950s & 1960s (O'Neil)
Motor Racing at Oulton Park in the 1960s (McFadyen)
Motor Racing at Oulton Park in the 1970s (McFadyen)
Motor Racing at Thruxton in the 1970s (Grant-Braham)
Motor Racing at Thruxton in the 1980s (Grant-Braham)
Superprix – The Story of Birmingham Motor Race (Page
 & Collins)
Three Wheelers (Bobbitt)

Rally Giants Series
Audi Quattro (Robson)
Austin Healey 100-6 & 3000 (Robson)
Fiat 131 Abarth (Robson)
Ford Escort MkI (Robson)
Ford Escort RS Cosworth & World Rally Car (Robson)
Ford Escort RS1800 (Robson)
Lancia Delta 4WD/Integrale (Robson)
Lancia Stratos (Robson)
Mini Cooper/Mini Cooper S (Robson)
Peugeot 205 T16 (Robson)
Saab 96 & V4 (Robson)

Subaru Impreza (Robson)
Toyota Celica GT4 (Robson)

General
1½-litre GP Racing 1961-1965 (Whitelock)
Alfa Romeo 155/156/147 Competition Touring Cars
 (Collins)
Alpine & Renault – The Development of the
 Revolutionary Turbo F1 Car 1968 to 1979 (Smith)
Alpine & Renault – The Sports Prototypes 1963 to 1969
 (Smith)
Alpine & Renault – The Sports Prototypes 1973 to 1978
 (Smith)
Bahamas Speed Weeks, The (O'Neil)
Bluebird CN7 (Stevens)
BMC Competitions Department Secrets (Turner,
 Chambers & Browning)
British at Indianapolis, The (Wagstaff)
BRM – A Mechanic's Tale (Salmon)
BRM V16 (Ludvigsen)
Carrera Panamericana, La (Tipler)
Chevrolet Corvette (Starkey)
Chrysler 300 – America's Most Powerful Car 2nd Edition
 (Ackerson)
Chrysler PT Cruiser (Ackerson)
Cobra – The Real Thing! (Legate)
Cobra, The last Shelby – My times with Carroll Shelby
 (Theodore)
Competition Car Aerodynamics 3rd Edition
 (McBeath)
Competition Car Composites A Practical Handbook
 (Revised 2nd Edition) (McBeath)
Cortina – Ford's Bestseller (Robson)
Cosworth – The Search for Power (6th edition) (Robson)
Coventry Climax Racing Engines (Hammill)
Daily Mirror 1970 World Cup Rally 40, The (Robson)
Dino – The V6 Ferrari (Long)
Dodge Challenger & Plymouth Barracuda (Grist)
Dodge Charger – Enduring Thunder (Ackerson)
Dodge Dynamite! (Grist)
Dodge Viper (Zatz)
Driven – An Elegy to Cars, Roads & Motorsport (Aston)
Fast Ladies – Female Racing Drivers 1888 to 1970
 (Bouzanquet)
Ferrari 288 GTO, The Book of the (Sackey)
Ferrari 333 SP (O'Neil)
Fiat & Abarth 124 Spider & Coupé (Tipler)
Fiat & Abarth 500 & 600 – 2nd Edition (Bobbitt)

Ford Cleveland 335-Series V8 engine 1970 to 1982 – The
 Essential Source Book (Hammill)
Ford F100/F150 Pick-up 1948-1996 (Ackerson)
Ford F150 Pick-up 1997-2005 (Ackerson)
Ford Focus WRC (Robson)
Ford GT – Then, and Now (Streather)
Ford GT40 (Legate)
Ford Midsize Muscle – Fairlane, Torino & Ranchero
 (Cranswick)
Ford Model Y (Roberts)
Ford Mustang II & Pinto 1970 to 80 (Cranswick)
Ford Small Block V8 Racing Engines 1962-1970 – The
 Essential Source Book (Hammill)
Ford Thunderbird From 1954, The Book of the (Long)
Ford versus Ferrari – The battle for supremacy at Le
 Mans 1966 (Starkey)
Formula 1 - The Knowledge 2nd Edition (Hayhoe)
Formula 1 All The Races - The First 1000 (Smith)
Formula One – The Real Score? (Harvey)
Formula 5000 Motor Racing, Back then ... and back now
 (Lawson)
The Good, the Mad and the Ugly ... not to mention
 Jeremy Clarkson (Dron)
Grand Prix Ferrari – The Years of Enzo Ferrari's Power,
 1948-1980 (Pritchard)
Grand Prix Ford – DFV-powered Formula 1 Cars
 (Robson)
GT – The World's Best GT Cars 1953-73 (Dawson)
Hillclimbing & Sprinting – The Essential Manual (Short
 & Wilkinson)
Jaguar E-type Factory and Private Competition Cars
 (Griffiths)
Kris Meeke – Intercontinental Rally Challenge
 Champion (McBride)
KTM X-Bow (Pathmanathan)
Lamborghini Miura Bible, The (Sackey)
Lamborghini Murciélago, The book of the
 (Pathmanathan)
Lamborghini Urraco, The Book of the (Landsem)
Lancia 037 (Collins)
Lancia Delta HF Integrale (Blaettel & Wagner)
Lancia Delta Integrale (Collins)
Le Mans Panoramic (Ireland)
Lola – The Illustrated History (1957-1977) (Starkey)
Lola – All the Sports Racing & Single-seater Racing Cars
 1978-1997 (Starkey)
Lola T70 – The Racing History & Individual Chassis
 Record – 4th Edition (Starkey)

Lotus 18 Colin Chapman's U-turn (Whitelock)
Lotus 49 (Oliver)
Lotus Elan and Plus 2 Source Book (Vale)
Maserati 250F In Focus (Pritchard)
Monthléry, The Story of the Paris Autodrome (Boddy)
MOPAR Muscle – Barracuda, Dart & Valiant 1960-1980
 (Cranswick)
Motor Racing – Reflections of a Lost Era (Carter)
Motor Racing – The Pursuit of Victory 1930-1962
 (Carter)
Motor Racing – The Pursuit of Victory 1963-1972
 (Wyatt/Sears)
Motor Racing Heroes – The Stories of 100 Greats
 (Newman)
Motorsport In colour, 1950s (Wainwright)
N.A.R.T. – A concise history of the North American
 Racing Team 1957 to 1983 (O'Neil)
Nissan GT-R Supercar: Born to race (Gorodji)]
Nissan – The GTP & Group C Racecars 1984-1993
 (Starkey)
Northeast American Sports Car Races 1950-1959
 (O'Neil)
Pontiac Firebird – New 3rd Edition (Cranswick)
Porsche 914 & 914-6: The Definitive History of the Road
 & Competition Cars (Long)
Porsche Racing Cars – 1953 to 1975 (Long)
Porsche Racing Cars – 1976 to 2005 (Long)
Porsche - Silver Steeds (Smith)
Porsche – The Rally Story (Meredith)
Powered by Porsche (Smith)
RAC Rally Action! (Gardiner)
Racing Colours – Motor Racing Compositions 1908-
 2009 (Newman)
Racing Mustangs – An International Photographic
 History 1964-1986 (Holmes)
Rallye Sport Fords: The Inside Story (Moreton)
Runways & Racers (O'Neil)
Sauber-Mercedes – The Group C Racecars 1985-1991
 (Starkey)
SM – Citroën's Maserati-engined Supercar (Long &
 Claverol)
Speedway – Auto racing's ghost tracks (Collins &
 Ireland)
This Day in Automotive History (Corey)
Two Summers – The Mercedes-Benz W196R Racing Car
 (Ackerson)
TWR Story, The – Group A (Hughes & Scott)
TWR's Le Mans Winning Jaguars (Starkey)

See our other imprints for a great
selection of special interest, animal
care and children's books

www.veloce.co.uk

First published in April 2020, this paperback edition published October 2020 by Veloce Publishing Limited, Veloce House, Parkway Farm Business Park, Middle Farm Way, Poundbury, Dorchester DT1 3AR, England. Tel +44 (0)1305 260068 / Fax 01305 250479 / e-mail info@veloce.co.uk / web www.veloce.co.uk or www.velocebooks.com.
ISBN: 978-1-787117-35-8 / UPC: 6-36847-01735-4.

MADE IN AMERICA! 🇺🇸

RACING
MUSTANGS

An International Photographic History
1964-1986

Steve Holmes

VELOCE PUBLISHING
THE PUBLISHER OF FINE AUTOMOTIVE BOOKS

CONTENTS

ABOUT THIS BOOK

Racing Mustangs, An International Photographic History 1964-1986, is a celebration of the first two decades of the Ford Mustang in road racing competition. This is a photographic book accompanied by words, and not a word book accompanied by photos. That being said, I've tried to provide enough technical detail on the Mustang and its evolution, to tie together the photographs featured in each chapter.

Although the Mustang competed in a broad range of competition programs that included rallying, speedway, and drag racing, I've focused almost exclusively on the model's road racing pedigree. To add other disciplines runs the risk of watering down the content too much. And really, Ford Motor Company placed greater emphasis on road racing than anything else.

Also, while the Mustang has enjoyed an almost unbroken racing history that began in 1964, this book concentrates on the early years, when Ford was actively involved in supporting the model in various road racing programs. Significantly, those years spanned 1964-1970. Determining the book's starting point was easy: start at the beginning. But choosing where to end was a lot more challenging, given the Mustang has been in production for over 50 years. I didn't want the book to meander without purpose. After all, its true focus is the early years, and everything else is a back-story. I settled on 1986 as the end-date. Having drifted just about as far from its original form as it was possible to go during the tube-frame/silhouette era of the late 1970s and early 1980s, the Mustang returned to international production-based racing in the European FIA Group A formula in the mid-1980s. Ford had no interest in Group A, but in many respects the Mustang had gone almost full-circle to where it had been two decades earlier in Group 2.

Furthermore, while this is an international book featuring racing Mustangs from around the world, it really centers around the most significant programs where Ford placed greatest importance, those being 1965 SCCA B/Production racing, and SCCA Trans-Am Championship from 1966-1970. No question, the Trans-Am was not only the biggest and greatest sedan racing series on the planet during this era, it was also one of the greatest and most significant motorsport spectacles of any kind. The rise in popularity of sedan racing in other parts of the world during the late 1960s can be directly attributed to the success of the Trans-Am.

Although Ford quit the Trans-Am series at the end of 1970, the Trans-Am itself continued on through 1972 in much the same guise. And, as such, to a lesser extent I've also included 1971 and 1972, as independent Ford racers battled on, regardless. For them, nothing had changed. Likewise, in countries such as Australia, Ford's US racing involvement, or lack thereof, had no influence on either the quality of racing, or the dedication of the racers.

As a whole, sedan racing changed from 1973. There was no longer an international sedan formula that united the world's sedan championships, as Group 2 had done in the 1960s. Furthermore, sedan racing lost its link with the road cars on which the racers were increasingly loosely based. Cars began sporting tube-frame chassis, over which were draped silhouette bodies that bore little similarity to their production counterparts. Although seemingly unrelated to the theme of this book, I felt it important to include this later period, if fleetingly, to show how the sport had evolved, and the role Mustang played within it.

By and large, this is a book that celebrates the period 1964-1970, when the Mustang gave rise to the pony car market, and was responsible for the greatest era in production-based sedan racing the world has ever seen.

I hope you enjoy the read.

Steve Holmes

ACKNOWLEDGMENTS

This book would never have been possible without the incredible help and support of countless contributors. First and foremost, I have to thank my good friend Chad Raynal, whose knowledge of the original 1966-1972 Trans-Am series and the cars that raced in it, right down to the finest of detail, continues to amaze me. I must have driven Chad nuts with my constant barrage of questions, but he never showed it once, and always appeared happy to help.

Rick Kopec of the Shelby American Automobile Club was another who I leaned on heavily, gathering information and photos of the early Shelby GT350 build processes and racing histories.

Thanks also to the incredible generosity of those who so kindly offered their photo collections, which helped to pull this whole project together. My thanks to Michael Keyser (Austosportsltd.com), Ron Lathrop, John Stanley, Rick Kopec at SAAC, Wayne Hill, Raynald Bélanger, Bruce Wells, Derek Sutton, Doug Morton, John Webber, Claudia McGhee, John Gauerke, Yves St-Jean, Dominic St-Jean (autocourse.ca), Randy Hernandez, Cliff Reuter, Ed Struke, Steve Twist, Forrest K Bond, Curtis Ross Wheatley, Charlie Kemp, Nick De Vitis, Jim Culp, Martin Beaulieu, Phil Rhodes, Perry Drury, Allan Cameron, Ross Cammick, Graeme Swan, Denis Giguere, Brad Leach, Walt Hane and Chris Wiehle.

My thanks to John Gabrial who shared his beautiful collection of Trans-Am program covers, and Pauly Baldacchino for the 1965 Sports Car Graphic cover.

Thanks to Wolfgang Korn for making available his incredible website ponysite.de, which shares Wolfgang's amazing research on the histories of so many first-generation racing Mustangs from around the world.

Thanks to the late Frank de Jong whose website touringcarracing.net features an enormous number of period sedan race results and information from around the world.

Thanks also to Gary Horstkorta, Brian Darby, Lee Dykstra, Jon Mello, Lindsay Ross, Mike Hayward, Robert Clayson, Dave Friedman, Revs Institute, Bernard from Mexico, Pat Mo, for providing information, connections, and more photos. Thanks also to Tim Nevinson, Becky Martin and the team at Veloce Publishing for making it possible to create this book in the first place. Thanks to my parents Marianne and Glenn for making me the race car fanatic I am. It's an illness!

Finally, thank you to my amazing, understanding wife, Helen, who has put up with me and my old race car obsession for years, and who barely saw me during the final couple of months that this project came together.

INTRODUCTION

It was the right car introduced at precisely the right time. And not just for Ford Motor Company, but for the American automotive industry as a whole. The Ford Mustang was a game-changer. It shifted the parameters of what an affordable car could offer. It set new sales records and generated unprecedented consumer excitement. And it kick-started an entirely new market segment.

And yet, had fate not intervened, it could so easily have never happened.

Robert McNamara had deservedly soared up through the Ford Motor Company ranks, from one of the 'Whiz Kids' of the late 1940s who helped overturn its lagging fortunes, to president in November 1960. He was the first non-Ford family member to achieve this feat.

Despite the opulence and dynamism that surrounded the automotive industry in the late 1950s, American manufacturers faced an uncertain future heading into the 1960s. A new generation of buyers was looming large on the horizon, dubbed the 'baby boomer' generation, and it was perhaps the most important yet. These were the sons and daughters of World War II veterans, born just after the war, and they displayed a unique buying pattern to that of their parents and previous generations. Style, sex appeal, image and individuality were important to the boomers, and US automotive manufacturers were aware that, by around 1960, they'd be reaching driving age, and by around 1965, they'd be in the market for new cars.

By 1960 it was recognized that around half of all new car sales would go to buyers under the age of 25 in the years to come, and that manufacturers needed to have a vehicle ready for these buyers when the time came. Predicting what that vehicle should be, however, created divisions within the ranks of every automaker, Ford Motor Company included.

Some within Ford were pushing for a sporty four-seater, with its own unique styling that distinguished it from everything else on the market. Others, McNamara among them, strongly believed a more sobering economy car was the answer. Indeed, so convinced was McNamara, that he gave approval to begin tooling, and, ultimately, large-scale production of the Cardinal, a conservatively-styled but relatively advanced small sedan powered by a tiny water-cooled V4 motor.

McNamara had barely got his feet under the table at the head of Ford when President John F Kennedy came knocking, and within weeks of him becoming president of Ford Motor Company, McNamara accepted the position of Secretary of Defense for the United States Government.

McNamara's departure prompted the promotion into the positions of Vice-President and General Manager of the Ford Division of 36-year-old Lee Iacocca. And it was under Iacocca that wholesale changes were made within Ford Motor Company during the 1960s, and the way it marketed its brand. Firstly, the Cardinal was cancelled. It did, in fact, see large-scale production in Germany, launched in 1962 as the Taunus 12 M. Focus, therefore, turned towards pre-empting the needs of the boomers.

Unlike McNamara, Iacocca believed the solution to the upcoming baby boomer conundrum was a personalized affordable sporty four-seater. As such, he began pushing ahead with plans to produce such a car, despite some internal resistance. Being able to personalize one's car was a luxury traditionally afforded only to the very top end of the market. Iacocca envisioned a car whose base price started at around $2500, but which its owner could option up, as they wished, and as their personality and budget allowed. To keep costs down, it was based on the existing Falcon platform, and would share some of its running gear and other appointments. It was important there be no obvious visual link between the two: after all, the Falcon's image was already cast as a budget-focused economy car, and, as such, a sporty new body shape was crafted. Buyers could choose between a notchback, convertible, and eventually a fastback body style.

By late 1963, Ford toured a Mustang prototype around the country to gauge public reaction. The response was largely positive. Leading up to its April 17, 1964 launch at the New York World's Fair, Ford began ramping up promotion, taking out full page adverts in over 2500 newspapers across the nation. These were coincided with a television advertising campaign. Each of the more than 8000 Ford dealerships were sent a Mustang prior to launch date. During the week before launch, 70 Mustangs were made available to over 100 members of the press, for a 700-mile (roughly 1120km) New York to Dearborn drive, in which each vehicle made the trek without issue, and with positive reviews.

It was Henry Ford II himself who introduced the Mustang at the 1964 New York World's Fair. Interest was overwhelming. Following its launch, an estimated 4 million people stormed Ford dealerships in the first week to view and test drive the new car. That same week both *Time* and *Newsweek* magazines featured the Mustang on their front covers. Iacocca suggests these stories alone helped contribute to 100,000 extra Mustang sales.

From its April 17 launch, Mustang sales topped 100,000 within the first four months, and over 680,000 had been sold by the end of 1965. One year on, this number had exceeded 1.3 million. 1966 was to be the model's best-ever year, with more than 607,000 sold. Mustang accounted for over 28% of total Ford sales during this period. Very quickly a second Mustang assembly plant had to be opened, this one in San Jose, California, to cater to demand.

When the Mustang hit the market, it did so as Ford Motor Company had just stepped up its already immense international motorsport program. In 1964, Ford was racing the new GT40 at Le Mans, the Ford Galaxie and Lincoln-Mercury division Marauder in NASCAR stock car racing, the Ford Fairlane and Mercury Comet in NHRA drag racing, and the Ford Falcon and Mercury Marauder in endurance rallying. As such, the new Mustang was to be incorporated into Ford's overall racing program.

In 1957, the Automobile Manufacturers Association, consisting of members representing major American automotive companies, agreed a withdrawal from all forms of motorsport. This agreement was largely self-imposed, citing fears that had they not done so themselves, Congress may have intervened and forced their hand.

What prompted the no-racing policy was a spate of fatalities of both drivers and spectators at racing events. The most devastating of these was the 1955 Le Mans 24 Hours tragedy, where a fast-closing Pierre Levegh's Mercedes 300SLR ploughed into Lance Macklin's Austin-Healey along the start/finish straight, launching the Mercedes into a spectator area at well over 100mph, where it disintegrated, showering the crowd in debris as it did so. Levegh and 83 spectators were killed, and over 180 more were injured. Mercedes-Benz, who was also fielding a successful Formula 1 campaign at the time, immediately withdrew from all forms of racing.

With fatalities in domestic racing being relatively common, the AMA feared a negative backlash through association from the use of motorsport to promote speed and horsepower, and ultimately, to help drive car sales. Inevitably, it felt, Congress would turn its sights on auto manufacturers, and inflict limitations involved with racing that could be far more drastic than anything it could impose on itself. So, it opted instead to take control of the situation.

The problem was, however, motorsport was a highly effective tool for selling cars. Racing created excitement associated with a brand, and media interest further elevated brand exposure. Additionally, the developments gained from a racing program also helped improve the blood-line. The National Association for Stock Car Auto Racing (NASCAR) had emerged among the countless grass-roots speedway associations littering the country, and its president and founder, Bill France, was fast gaining a reputation as a visionary who could take grand ideas and bring them to life. While speedway racing was built upon a foundation of feral prewar Modified cars, NASCAR included, France sought to engage the auto manufacturers, and established a new division called Strictly Stock, which catered to modern cars of the types being sold in dealer show rooms. Strictly Stock was quickly re-branded as NASCAR Grand National, and its march to prominence was swift.

France had ambition far beyond the gritty little bull-ring dirt ovals on the outskirts of every small town across the country. He wanted to polish the sport, make it more accepted, and more appealing to the auto industry, the media, and the fans. This he achieved by building glittering new motorsport facilities, which were triumphant structures in their own right. On February 6, 1959, 42,000 people attended the first Daytona 500 at France's colossal new 3.5-mile banked superspeedway, where race cars reached speeds previously unheard of in stock car racing. Two years later, that figure rose by another 10,000. And so the trend continued year-on-year.

To have in excess of 50,000 people assembled in one place to watch a car race couldn't be ignored. France was making NASCAR so successful the automotive industry needed to be involved in some way. And indeed, they were, despite the self-imposed AMA racing ban.

In truth, the manufacturers never really withdrew from racing. Their support of teams and drivers became covert, and they were cautious in how they capitalized on racing accomplishments. They'd supply cars, parts, and technical assistance to selected teams, and success from those efforts generated sales. It was all a smoke-screen, of course. But emotion drives sales, and racing drives emotion, and automotive manufacturers are in the business of selling cars. By the early 1960s, the game was up.

In 1962, Ford Motor Company was the first to openly withdraw from the AMA no-racing policy. Once the shackles were off, it came out swinging for the fences. It went at racing with total commitment, spending whatever it took to succeed at whatever form of racing it had in the cross-hairs. This was Total Performance, indeed, and Ford branded it as such.

As its new sporty car, the Mustang had to fit into Ford's Total Performance marketing program – so it had to go racing. Its booming sales figures suggested a racing involvement wasn't an immediate priority; it was selling, regardless. But if imitation is the greatest form of flattery, the Mustang would very soon have plenty of company from Ford's opponents, its sales figures demanded as much.

Initially, the Mustang took the place of the Falcon in European endurance rallying. Gradually, the Falcon had been elevated from its original concept as a conservative economy car, built to tackle the VW Beetle, which genuinely had Detroit worried. It evolved throughout the early 1960s, culminating in the V8-powered Sprint. But with the Mustang now in the market, the Falcon quietly reverted back to its original role.

The Mustang rallying program was short-lived. Ford couldn't garner a lot of marketing clout from a racing exercise taking place half a world away. For 1965, it went racing in the Sports Car Club of America (SCCA) production sports car division, competing against the Corvette, where it triumphed. In 1966, recognizing a new pony car market was on the horizon thanks to the Mustang's sales success, the SCCA capitalized by launching the Trans-American Sedan Championship (Trans-Am), which would become the most prominent road racing sedan series anywhere in the world within two years of its inception.

By 1970, every large domestic car manufacturer in the United States was represented in the Trans-Am, and in their efforts to win, had produced road-going hot rods designed to homologate specific low-volume components to make their counterparts winners on the track – and they were spending millions for the privilege.

It wasn't just domestically that the Mustang became a prolific road racer, it also found favor internationally. Even before the SCCA had launched the Trans-Am Championship in 1966, Mustangs had already won both the British Saloon Car Championship and Australian Touring Car Championship in 1965, and the successes continued to snowball throughout the remainder of the decade.

Of course, it couldn't last, and it didn't. The Trans-Am series, much like that of the pony car market as a whole, fell into rapid decline in the early 1970s. Its demise was swift, and brutal. A combination of events; new horsepower-sapping Government smog regulations, escalating insurance costs on sporty cars, and fears of an impending energy crisis and fuel-shortages all played a part. But perhaps more-so was a natural shift in the market and its buyers, and what they wanted from their vehicles. The generation that gave life to the pony car market was itself superseded by the next generation, and its influential buying powers.

It was a short-lived era. But while it lasted, it was really something.

1964

Traditionally, automotive manufacturers unveil next year's new-car offerings late the preceding year, usually around September/October. Given the Mustang was brought to market on April 17, 1964, more-or-less six months outside the typical launch season, the early cars have always been referred to as 1964 ½ models. Regardless, they are fitted with 1965 VIN tags.

When the Mustang came to market, Ford's 1964 competition program was already in full-swing, and rather than try to shoe-horn it into a mid-year campaign, all efforts instead channeled towards 1965. In truth, the new Mustang was fresh and exciting enough, and different enough to anything currently on the market, that promoting it through motorsport wasn't so important. Initially, at least, Ford was kept busy just producing enough cars to meet demand. The great underlying factor for any automotive manufacturer, or any business for that matter, is plain old dollars and cents. Upon launch, the Mustang's spectacular sales figures demanded Ford's rivals would very quickly react, and bring their own versions of the pony car to market. And that's where a racing program has its benefits. Nothing stimulates emotion, brand loyalty, and sets apart one brand from another quite like motor racing. Even in April 1964, Ford was already working towards an ambitious 1965 racing program.

Ford did, however, involve itself in a 1964 competition program of sorts, although most Americans likely wouldn't have been aware of it. In late 1962 the company embarked on an unlikely project to race its upcoming Falcon Sprint in European endurance rallies. These bruising contests spanned several days, scaling mountain roads in ice and snow, combined with white-knuckle, foot to the boards sections along paved and unpaved public roads.

Holman Moody was tasked with building a fleet of Falcon Sprints to contest the 1963 Monte Carlo Rally, held from January 20-24. The Holman Moody-prepared Falcons were then shipped to Alan Mann Racing, Ford's Great Britain competition team, who prepared and raced them. Against smaller, more nimble European cars, better suited to the roads and

conditions, the Falcons performed surprisingly well. Swedish rally star Bosse 'Bo' Ljungfeldt proved a stand-out, winning several stages, but ultimately finished well down the order due to traffic delays caused by ice and snow on the mountain roads. However, French rally driver Henri Greder drove one of the Alan Mann Falcons to victory in the Tulip Rally, held from April 22-26.

For the 1964 Monte Carlo Rally, held from January 18-21, Holman Moody built a new batch of the latest wedge-shaped Falcon Sprints, which were homologated with the FIA at an optimistically low 980kg (2160lb) minimum racing weight. To attempt this goal, the cars were fitted with fiberglass hoods, deck lids, front fenders, and doors, along with aluminum bumpers.

Formula 1 World Champion, Graham Hill, headed the driver line-up, but again it was the fleet-footed Ljungfeldt who spearheaded the Ford charge, winning several of the special stages, and finishing second overall, behind Paddy Hopkirk in a BMC Mini Cooper, from an entry of 210 cars.

In February, 1964, Alan Mann Racing received a prototype Mustang which was immediately put to work as a test-mule, from which a detailed report was sent back to Detroit. This car was also used to homologate the model with the Fédération Internationale de l'Automobile (FIA) for competition use. The FIA rejected the first application, placed in June, using Recognition Number 1329, on the basis that Ford Special Vehicles Manager Jacque Passino and Ford Rally Competition Manager George Merwin had signed the accompanying paperwork as mere managers. In effect, the FIA considered they weren't important enough. To that end, the very same forms were resubmitted in July, this time with Passino and Merwin listed as Directors. The FIA approved, and the Mustang was now homologated for racing. It was granted FIA Recognition Number 1330, beginning with chassis number 5F07K-100001. Specifically, the stated chassis number included the letter K, this being the engine code for the Hi-Performance 271 horsepower 289in^3 V8.

Page 8 of the Mustang's homologation sheet reveals its formative competition outings were targeting European endurance rallying. Under

The Ford Mustang first went on sale on April 17, 1964, but almost immediately,owners were testing the capabilities of their brand new cars. This is Bob Acton at the May Spring Sprints in Waterford Hills, on May 30, 1964. For some of the spectators watching from the sidelines, this was possibly the first Mustang they'd ever seen. *(Courtesy Ron Lathrop Photos)*

'Optional Equipment' was listed, among various heavy-duty components, a 37-liter auxiliary fuel tank, and sump and fuel-tank guards. All items necessary for endurance rallying events.

Meanwhile, from a batch of pre-production Mustangs, five were sent to Europe in March, two of which were destined for Alan Mann Racing, where they'd be race-prepared for the models first official competition event, the Liège-Sofia-Liège Rally, held August 25-29. Because the event was contested on public roads, the cars had to be road-registered and given license plates: in this case, DPG3B and DPJ8B.

Both Mustangs crashed out of the gruelling event, which boasted a 3700 mile (roughly 6000km) distance from Belgium to the former Yugoslavia and back. Bo Ljungfeldt was driving DPJ8B, and crashed during a night stage when the headlights failed. The second car, driven by Peter Procter, suffered brake failure.

Meanwhile, in July, a further four Mustangs were shipped to Alan Mann Racing, where they were prepared for the 1964 Tour de France rally, contested September 11-20. These four cars, all of which were painted red, carried the VINs 5F07K208109, 5F07K208110, 5F07K208111, and 5F07K208112, and were registered DPK5B, DPK6B, DPK7B, and DPK4B. Three cars would contest the rally, these being 5B, 6B, and 7B, while 4B retained as the spare.

Compared to the Liège rally Mustangs, the Tour de France fleet were more heavily developed. They were powered by Holman Moody built 289in³ engines, and were constructed to withstand much harsher conditions. To accommodate heavy-duty steel wheels and large tires, and to absorb extensive suspension travel, their fenders were lightly flared.

Each of the 117 entries for the 1964 Tour de France had to fit into one of two categories; Touring or GT. The first seven finishing positions, predictably, were GT class cars; Ferrari 250 GTO's, Porsche 904's, and an Alfa Romeo Giulia TZ. But in eighth and ninth places outright, and first and second in the Touring class, were the Peter Procter and Peter Harper driven Alan Mann Racing Mustangs. The third Alan Mann Mustang, driven by Ljungfeldt, suffered electrical problems and was disqualified from the event. A fourth Mustang, entered by Ford France, and driven by Henri Greder, also failed to complete the distance.

The 1964 Tour de France signalled the end of Ford's official involvement in European endurance rallying that began with the Falcon Sprints in late 1962. It was, overall, a successful campaign, if a little obscure, but certainly, Ford did get some marketing mileage from it, and undoubtedly, would have gained valuable knowledge on the strengths and weaknesses of the Mustang in a competition setting.

From 1965, all official Mustang motorsport programs would focus on domestic road course racing.

When Ford first submitted its application to the FIA to homologate the Mustang in June 1964, it was rejected on account of Ford Special Vehicles Manager Jacque Passino and Ford Rally Competition Manager George Merwin signing off the paperwork as Managers. So it was resubmitted in July, this time with Passino and Merwin listed as Directors, and this time it was approved. Note the list of Optional Equipment homologated for the car. The Mustang was first homologated for rallying.

ORIGINAL   FIA

Telephone: (212) LExington 2-5521   Cable Address: "ACCUSFIA-NEW YORK"

AUTOMOBILE COMPETITION COMMITTEE FOR THE UNITED STATES, FIA, INC.

107 EAST 38th STREET, NEW YORK 16, N.Y.

FORM OF RECOGNITION IN ACCORDANCE WITH APPENDIX J TO THE INTERNATIONAL SPORTING CODE

Manufacturer's Reference No. for application   64507-K   FIA Recognition No.   1329

Manufacturer   FORD MOTOR COMPANY

Model   1965 MUSTANG Mk 1   Year of manufacture   1964

Serial No. of   Chassis starts with   5F07K-100001

Engine starts with   Same

Type of bodywork   Two-Door Hardtop

Recognition is valid from   11/7/64   In category Touring   Touring
(FIA to insert date)   or Grand Touring

liste 2/11

Stamp of ACCUS-FIA, INC. to be affixed here

Stamp of FIA to be affixed here   Signed _____ Sec'y

JUN 26 1964

-1-

1329

General description of car: (specifying materials of bodywork)

Two-Door welded body shell permanently attached to a platform
frame of welded steel construction.

(3/4 view of car from rear left.)

(Interior view of car through driver's door.)

(Engine unit with accessories from right.)

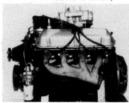

(Engine unit with accessories from left.)

(Front axle complete (without wheels).)

(Rear axle complete (without wheels).)

- 2 -

Optional equipment affecting preceeding information:-

Stamped pressed steel disc with 139.7 mm welded rim and 15 in. wheel.
Auxiliary fuel tank 37 liters.
~~Touring seats and interior trim.~~
Guard for sump and fuel tank.
Heavy duty springs and shock absorbers front and rear.
Spring lower supports

Alternate Axle Ratios. Ref. Page 5

Ratios	3.25	3.10	3.50	3.89	4.29
# Teeth Ring Gear	39	31	35	35	30
# Teeth Pinion	12	10	10	9	7

ORIGINAL   FIA

Telephone: (212) LExington 2-5521   Cable Address: "ACCUSFIA-NEW YORK"

AUTOMOBILE COMPETITION COMMITTEE FOR THE UNITED STATES, FIA, INC.

107 EAST 38th STREET, NEW YORK 16, N. Y.

FORM OF RECOGNITION IN ACCORDANCE WITH APPENDIX J TO THE INTERNATIONAL SPORTING CODE

Manufacturer's Reference No. for
application   64508-K   FIA Recognition No. 1330

Manufacturer FORD MOTOR COMPANY

Model 1965 MUSTANG Mk 2   Year of manufacture 1964

Serial No. of   Chassis starts with 5F07K-100001

Engine starts with Same

Type of bodywork Two-Door Hardtop

Recognition is valid from 11/7/64 In category Touring Touring
(FIA to insert date)   or Grand Touring

liste 2/11

Stamp of FIA to be
affixed here

Stamp of ACCUS-FIA, INC.
to be affixed here

Signed

JUN 26 1964

Alan Mann Racing entered three Mustangs in the 1964 Tour de France, held in September. Pictured here are DPK 6B, driven by Peter Harper, with David Pollard as co-driver, and DPK 7B, shared by Peter Procter and Andrew Cowan. Procter and Cowan won the Touring class, with Harper and Pollard second.

(Courtesy Revs Institute, Eric della Faille)

Following their duties in the 1964 Tour de France, the Alan Mann Mustangs went their separate ways. DPK 7B immediately returned to the US, and then to Canada, with the Comstock Racing Team. It was driven by Skip Scott at Nassau Speed Week in late November, still wearing its British license plate.

(Courtesy Revs Institute, Albert R Bochroch)

1965

This was it, then. Ford launched the Mustang into a domestic road racing program in 1965, with its exciting new Shelby GT350. The GT350 was the culmination of a concentrated program that extended throughout much of 1964. Indeed, the Shelby GT350 served to underline the total commitment Ford had to racing the Mustang.

The three different body styles and almost endless list of options available to Mustang customers meant this was a car to suit the needs of every buyer, and, in Ford's opinion, that included sports car buyers. Lee Iacocca wanted to take the Mustang sports car racing, but the problem was, it wasn't really a sports car. The Corvette was a sports car. The Mustang, however, was a sporty car. For a start, it had four seats. Ford didn't really have a true sports car in its arsenal, but Iacocca was determined. He wanted it spoken of in the same breath as the Corvette, Chevrolet's halo car, so he approached the nations leading road racing organization, the Sports Car Club of America, but his attempts were flatly rebuked. The SCCA declared the Mustang simply wasn't a sports car.

Resolute, Iacocca tackled the problem from a different angle, this time indirectly, through Carroll Shelby. Really, it was the perfect solution. Shelby was already working for Ford Motor Company. His Shelby Cobra sports cars were powered by Ford engines, and Ford provided funding for his racing efforts, including those in the World Sports Car Championship. Shelby was a big name in racing, a celebrity among racing celebrities. He'd built his reputation, both as a driver and manufacturer, through sports car racing, and he was held in high esteem throughout the racing community. He ran a slick operation, so his association with the new Mustang would help give it credibility as a sports car. Furthermore, Shelby already had his own cottage-industry production plant up and running, employing a small but highly skilled team of people building specialist sports cars in tiny numbers. Manufacture of a Mustang built for SCCA sports car racing would need to be out-sourced by Ford. Its massive assembly plants were only designed for large-scale production, and a custom-built Mustang sports car would be anything but.

Shelby's opinion of the Mustang reflected that of the SCCA, but he wisely took the project on. The result was the Shelby GT350.

The SCCA hosted divisions for both Modified and Production-based sports cars. The criteria for SCCA Production sports car racing was that the manufacturer produce a minimum 100 cars by January 1 of the year it wanted to go racing. For its Production categories, the SCCA used international FIA GT regulations. Furthermore, vehicles had to comply with certain conditions, among which they have no less and no more than two seats.

The SCCA employed an adjustable sliding-scale system for its Production sports car classes, which ranged from A/Production through to H/Production; A/Production being for the fastest cars, such as the Shelby Cobras and big block Corvettes. Cars were categorized through a mix of engine size and determined performance. The ideal outcome was one with a variety of makes and models of similar performance, all competing within the same class. If a model was deemed too fast, or too slow, it was moved up or down into the class best suited to it. The small block Corvettes, Sunbeam Tigers, Jaguar XKEs, and other cars of similar performance were grouped in B/Production. Once approved, they'd be joined by the Shelby GT350.

Provided at least 100 cars were built by the due date, it didn't matter if they were road or race cars. For the most-part, race teams had no option but to purchase road cars and convert them into race cars. In the case of the Shelby GT350, they wouldn't have to. As part of its production run, Shelby American would construct a small number of turn-key Shelby GT350 race cars. In total, 562 1965-model Shelby GT350s were produced, 36 of which were race-ready cars, while the remainder were road cars.

The Shelby GT350 race cars were just that; they could be ordered directly through a Ford dealer, were fully homologated, and could be taken

Early Shelby American promotional material featured both street and race cars. Pictured at LAX, this is almost certainly SFM5R002 and SFM5S003: the first street and race cars built. *(Courtesy SAAC)*

straight to the track and raced. Shelby American would campaign its own cars in 1965 SCCA B/Production sports car competition, and the customer cars were of the very same specification.

Ford's San Jose assembly plant would supply Shelby American with special-order batches of Wimbledon White, K-code Mustang fastbacks. Shelby American then converted them into Shelby GT350s, before dispatching them to Ford dealers around the country. When the GT350 program began, Shelby American was located in Venice, California, in a small collection of shops, and it was here the first handful of GT350s were built. But limited space meant only around eight or ten cars could be worked on at any one time, and the lack of a proper assembly-line made the whole process quite clumsy. Therefore, a new facility was located at Los Angeles International Airport, utilizing two huge aircraft hangars totalling 96,000 square feet on a 12.5 acre site, right alongside one of the runways. In one of the buildings, a long pit was dug, over which an assembly-line was constructed.

In late October, 1964, the first three Wimbledon White K-code fastback Mustangs were delivered from the San Jose plant to Shelby American. These would become Shelby GT350 prototypes. Two would be built as GT350 B/Production race cars, the third as a GT350 road car. These cars would serve as the templates that, for the most part, all other 1965-model Shelby GT350s would be replicated. Shelby American would themselves campaign the two race cars, while the road car was used for promotional and advertising purposes.

To minimize time and costs, the Mustangs were ordered and supplied with a number of deleted parts, of which Shelby American would fit its own custom-made variants as part of the transformation process. Both the street and race cars were supplied without a hood or rear seat. Deletions for the road cars were mostly decorative, such as trim pieces. Those destined to become race cars were ordered with a much longer list of deletions,

including front and rear bumpers, side and rear windows, side vents, interior upholstery, headliner, heater, defroster, insulation and sound-deadener. They were also ordered without the stamped steel "eyebrows" welded to the top of the dashboard to support the foam dash pad.

For the conversion process, cars were fitted with traction bars, which required cutting two holes in the floorplan and welding brackets to the floor and the rear axle housing onto which the bars were connected. Up front, the A-arms were removed, and new mounting holes were drilled, one inch higher than stock, which lowered the car's ride height. New idler and Pitman arms were installed, along with a 1in sway bar. This process took place on both the street and race cars.

All Shelby GT350s were fitted with a Borg-Warner T-10 four-speed gearbox and 9in differential with Detroit-locker limited slip, larger rear brake drums, and one-piece fiberglass hood with a central air-scoop.

While the road cars received an aluminum high-rise intake manifold, Holley 715CFM carburettor, aluminum oil pan and rocker covers, and tubular exhaust headers which boosted them from 271 to 306-horsepower, the race cars underwent a more intensive engine upgrade. This involved removing the engines, and sending the heads away to be ported, polished, and milled, giving a compression ratio of 12.0:1. Other upgrades included an S1CR racing camshaft, polishing and blueprinting of the rotating assembly, fitting of an aluminum Cobra high-rise intake manifold with ports matched to the heads, and steel tubular Tri-Y headers which connected to open exhausts,

Continues on page 21

(Pages 18-20) Shelby American made available every part required to convert a Shelby GT350 street car into a race car through its catalogue. Customers also purchased many of these parts to convert Mustang notchbacks into FIA Group 2 sedans. *(Courtesy SAAC)*

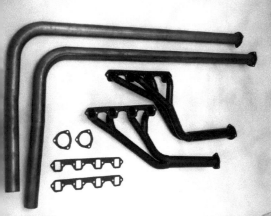

one exiting either side just in front of the rear wheels. Race engines typically produced around 350-horsepower.

For the race cars, a larger radiator was installed. This was a custom-made piece built by Modine specifically for Shelby American, and comprising parts from two different Galaxie radiators. The fuel tank was essentially the bottom halves of two stock 16-gallon Mustang tanks welded together, providing a 32-gallon capacity. It had a 3½in aluminum snap-open filler cap and a 10in diameter splash bucket.

As the race cars were delivered without the large rear window, the special four-point roll cage was lowered down through the window opening and bolted to the floor. The roll cage and a one-piece fiberglass shelf took up the space vacated by the rear seat. That's right: there was no rear seat – these were legitimate two-seater sports cars. An aluminum dash bezel was installed carrying a tachometer, speedometer, fuel pressure, oil temperature, oil pressure, and water temperature gauges. Thin aluminum door panels painted in semi-gloss black replaced the standard Mustang padded door panels.

The race cars required various bodywork modifications to the fender openings to house the 15x7in magnesium American Racing Wheels and chunky Goodyear racing tires.

A lot of attention went into weight reduction, and this included fitting a Plexiglass rear window, in which the top of the window didn't match the roof. This was the brainchild of Shelby American employee Pete Brock, who'd been responsible for the swoopy Cobra Daytona Coupe race cars. Brock's theory was that the gap would reduce both drag and interior air pressure. The vents normally fitted behind the side windows weighed 15lb each, so these were replaced on the race cars with a flat aluminum sheet, pop-riveted to the body. Plexiglass also replaced the glass side windows.

SCCA regulations allowed the removal of front and rear bumpers, but Shelby American went one step further by removing the steel lower front valance and replacing it with a fiberglass piece that featured a large central opening to duct air to the radiator and oil cooler, while a pair of smaller ducts either side snaked their way to the front brakes via 3in diameter flexible pipes. Brock originally designed rear brake ducts on either side of the bodywork just in front of the rear wheel openings. These were covered by modified Cobra hood scoops, to force air to the ducts, but they didn't make the final cut on the 1965 cars. Instead, small underbody scoops were employed.

After the first three prototypes had been completed, Project Engineer Chuck Cantwell paid a visit to the San Jose assembly plant, during which he discovered the Export Brace, a triangular steel brace fitted to Mustangs destined for export, to help support the shock towers on rough roads. Recognizing that these braces would be beneficial to the race cars, he included them on the order sheet for Mustangs being shipped to Shelby American. Export Braces were added retrospectively to both prototype race cars, and all subsequent road and race cars, but the prototype road car was never fitted with one. In addition, a tubular fender-to-fender Monte Carlo bar was attached, so-called because it had been fitted to the Ford entries on the European rallies. The Export Brace and Monte Carlo bar provided a strong triangular support that added rigidity to the front-end of the GT350s.

Pete Brock designed the Shelby GT350 color scheme, which celebrated American racing history and American international racing heroes of the past, including Briggs Cunningham and Lucky Casner. Guardsman Blue rocker stripes with 'GT350' lettering ran along the lower side bodywork between the front and rear wheels. Two 10in wide Guardsman Blue Le Mans stripes, running front the rear along the top, could be special-ordered. Less than a third of 1965-model Shelby GT350s were ordered with Le Mans stripes.

When K-code Mustangs were converted to Shelby GT350s, they were assigned a new Shelby American VIN tag, which was pop-riveted over the Ford VIN stamped to the inner splash-panel. 1965 cars used the VIN starting

with SFM5001 (Shelby Ford Mustang 1965 chassis 001). The Shelby numbers related to their processing at Shelby American, and not their original Ford VINs. The fourth car built was tagged SFM5004, and this was to be the first customer car.

After 31 cars had been built, someone at Shelby noted they were actually making two versions of the GT350; a Street model and a Race model, and that the VIN tags should probably reflect this. So street cars included an S in the VIN, and race cars an R. Therefore, car number 32, the first to include the new designation in its VIN, was tagged SFM5S032, denoting this a street car. The production number sequence wasn't affected by this. The first race car to include the new R designation was the 94th GT350 built, and was therefore given the VIN tag SFM5R094.

Of the three prototypes, the street car was the first to be built, followed by the two race cars. Initially, none of these cars received Shelby VIN tags, and it was loosely decided that when they did, it would be in the order they were converted. When this eventually happened, which took place in the Shelby parts department, the person stamping the tags did so in order of their Ford VINs, which meant the street car was tagged SFM5S003, the first race car built was tagged SFM5R002, and the second race car built, which had the lowest Ford VIN, was tagged SFM5R001.

John Bishop, SCCA Executive Director, visited Shelby American in early January, 1965, to check on production figures. Although far short of the requisite number to gain approval, he was satisfied all requirements would be met. That there were over 100 hoodless white Mustang fastbacks at the Shelby American facility awaiting conversion no doubt helped convince him the operation was legitimate, and he approved the Shelby GT350s eligibility to contest the SCCA B/Production division in 1965.

Years later, in the early 1970s when early Shelby GT350s started becoming collectors'-items, enthusiasts began referring to the Shelby American-built

race cars as R-models. However, when new, most people, the media included, invariably called them 'competition models.'

The name Shelby GT350 has no technical or performance relation to the actual cars. Significant time had passed as the project rumbled along throughout 1964, and various names for the model had been mooted, and rejected. These included Mustang Cobra, Shelby Cobra Mustang, Cobra Mustang GT, among others. Finally, Carroll Shelby asked Shelby American engineer and all-round problem-solver Phil Remington what he thought to be the distance between the company's Princeton Street and Carter Street buildings in Venice, from which it operated. Remington's answer; roughly 350 feet. To that end, Shelby announced the car would be named the GT350.

The Shelby GT350 made its race debut at Green Valley Raceway, in Smithfield, Texas, on February 14, 1965. Texan Carroll Shelby wanted the car to make its first competition appearance in front of his home crowd. Chassis SFM5R002 was driven by Ken Miles, who won his B/Production class.

In 1965, the SCCA divided its territory into six regions. Each region conducted its own series of points-paying races, spread across the year. At the conclusion of those races, the driver with the most points in each class was crowned Divisional Champion. The six Divisional Champions from around the country, plus the second and third placed drivers in regional points, were then invited to compete at a single year-end event, held at a venue that alternated from the East Coast to the West Coast. This event was called the American Road Race of Champions (ARRC), and the winner from each class would be crowned SCCA National Champion.

The 1965 ARRC was contested at Daytona International Speedway, utilizing the road course layout designed to the host the annual 24 Hours sports car race. Following its debut at Green Valley, the Shelby American GT350 was driven throughout the remaining Divisional races by Sports Car Graphic Editor Jerry Titus. Initially, Titus drove 5R002, but stepped aboard

Opposite: Green Valley Raceway. The all-new Shelby GT350 made its competition debut at Green Valley Raceway, in Texas, on February 14, 1965. This was important to Texan Carroll Shelby. Ken Miles was at the wheel of SFM5R002, which won its B/Production class on debut.

(Courtesy Jerry Melton/etceterini.com)

Green Valley Raceway. Carroll Shelby accompanied the new Shelby GT350 to Green Valley, and was surrounded by fans throughout.

(Courtesy Jerry Melton/etceterini.com)

the newly-completed 5R001 when it became available. Chuck Cantwell took over 5R002 in selected races to help create a points-buffer between Titus and his nearest rivals.

The Shelby American SCCA B/Production program was a tiny operation. Carroll Shelby was heavily committed to racing both the Ford GT40 and Cobra Daytona Coupe in FIA international events in 1965, so the B/Production program became a combined effort between Shelby American and Hi Performance Motors, owned by racer Lew Spencer.

Titus went on to become 1965 Division 6 (Pacific Coast) Champion, which qualified him for the ARRC.

There was a total of ten Shelby GT350s entered for the 1965 ARRC, including the Shelby American 5R002 for Chuck Cantwell. Cantwell hadn't amassed enough points to qualify, but in the event one of those that did couldn't attend, others from the same division would be granted a berth. He didn't get to start, however. Among the other GT350 entries were two converted S-model cars.

The B/Production grid was combined with A/Production, although each driver was only in competition with cars from their class. The fastest B/Production car was the Shelby GT350 of Mark Donohue (SFM5R105), who qualified on the front row of the combined grid, splitting the Shelby Cobras of Hal Keck and George Montgomery. Donohue had carried out various developments on his car, changing springs and shocks, and sway-bars. He also lowered the nose and fitted 8.5in wide American Racing drag wheels on the rear, with huge Firestone tires.

While Donohue was quickest, his race ended early with a blown tire. The loads being placed on the suspension around the banked speedway sections of the track were pressing the outside rear tire into the rear leaf springs. Donohue and his crew discovered the problem during practice and ground away some of the spring metal, but it wasn't enough. His tire

blew on lap 18 of the 25-lap race, handing the win, and the B/Production National Championship, to Titus, who was running second at the time. Bob Johnson, driving another Shelby GT350, finished second, and Don Yenko, in a Corvette, was third.

Although anyone with $5995.00 could order a Shelby GT350 race car, all parts used for R-model conversion were made available to purchase through Shelby American's catalogue, including complete race motors. And subsequently, many people purchased all, or a selection of these parts and performed their own conversions, mostly to S-model Shelby GT350s.

However, Shelby American had many international customers buying R-model parts for fitting to Mustang notchbacks. In 1965, Mustang notchbacks raced in the British Saloon Car Championship, European Touring Car Championship, Australian Touring Car Championship, and New Zealand Saloon Car Championship, as well as various other domestic sedan championships. These sedan championships were all contested to FIA Group 2 regulations, in which the notchback models shared a number of mechanical similarities to the B/Production R-model Shelby GT350s.

Green Valley Raceway. Bill Steele runs off-course in his A/Production Cobra as Ken Miles ducks down the inside. *(Courtesy Jerry Melton/etceterini.com)*

Green Valley Raceway. This hump on one of the straights allowed Miles to get the GT350 up off the deck. Very quickly, photographers gathered to capture the moment each time he powered by. Shelby American famously used a photo of the airborne Shelby in press-releases and advertising. *(Courtesy Jerry Melton/etceterini.com)*

For the 1965 British Saloon Car Championship, Alan Mann Racing converted its 1964 Tour de France Mustangs to FIA Group 2 regulations, and sold them off. One of these cars was raced by Roy Pierpoint, who went on to win the 1965 BSCC.

Meanwhile, Australian racers Norm Beechey, Ian Geoghegan, and Bob Jane all built Mustang notchbacks fitted with various Shelby GT350 R-model parts, as did New Zealand racer Ivan Segedin. The Australian Touring Car Championship was contested as a single race, hosted in 1965 at Calder Park Raceway, in Victoria. Jane qualified his Mustang on pole position, but Beechey drove through the field after a troubled qualifying session to win. Segedin raced his Mustang in New Zealand, finishing third in the New Zealand Group 2 Championship.

As a road racer, the Mustang had truly arrived.

Australia. Norm Beechey (center) was the first to race a Mustang in Australia, in January 1965. His car won the 1965 Australian Touring Car Championship. The Australian Mustangs used a Cobra competition intake manifold with four Weber carburettors. *(Courtesy John Stanley (color) and Bruce Wells)*

Australia. This is Bob Jane's Australian Mustang. Its first race was the Australian Touring Car Championship in April 1965. He qualified fastest, but retired from the race with overheating. This car was destroyed in November 1965 when a rear axle broke at Catalina Park, and it barrel-rolled along the safety fence. *(Courtesy Bruce Wells)*

Australia. Ian Geoghegan debuted his Mustang in August 1965. This very quickly became the fastest racing sedan in Australia, and won the 1966 Australian Touring Car Championship. It's pictured here at Catalina Park.

(Courtesy Bruce Wells)

One of the very first Shelby GT350s to be raced was the Hayward Ford car driven by Dick Carter. This is chassis SFM5019, the 19th car built. It was purchased in March 1965, before the first production R-models were available. It was built as a street car and converted to R-model specifications using parts supplied by Shelby American. *(Courtesy Carter family)*

The first production R-model Shelby GT350 was SFM5R094. Tom Yeager pre-ordered this car at Nassau, in December 1964, after speaking to Carroll Shelby about the upcoming model. It was shipped to Yeager on April 7, 1965. Yeager finished second in SCCA Division 3 points, and 6th at the 1965 ARRC at Daytona.

(Courtesy SAAC)

This is SFM5R096, pictured at Circuit Mont-Tremblant. It was the third R-model customer car, purchased by Comstock Racing Team, in Canada, and driven by Eppie Weitzes. It was adorned in the Comstock colors of white with dark green stripes. Comstock Racing fitted the car with Weber carburettors and Cobra intake manifold. Note the hump on the front of the hood. This was to allow fitment of a larger radiator and cap. (Courtesy Denis Giguere)

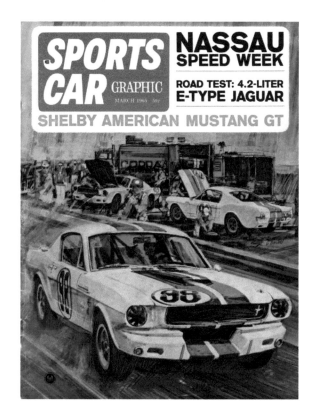

Pictured at Circuit Mont-Tremblant in July 1965 is the Comstock Racing Team Group 2 Mustang driven by Greg Fisher. (Courtesy Yves St-Jean)

Above and right: SFM5R097 was purchased by Georges Filipinetti, in Switzerland. It was the first GT350 R-model raced in Europe, and ran under the Scuderia Filipinetti banner. For the most-part, Scuderia Filipinetti raced Ferraris, which were painted in the Swiss racing colors red and white. As an acknowledgement of this, the Scuderia Filipinetti GT350 wore a thin red stripe between the two Le Mans stripes on the hood. (*Courtesy SAAC*)

SFM5R098 was the fifth R-model customer car. It was owned by Ned Owen, a good friend of Skip Scott, who drove a Cobra for the Essex Wire Corporation team in 1965. Essex Wire was a supplier to Ford Motor Company, and because of his close association with Ford, Scott received a 10% discount on Ford vehicles. Therefore, Scott ordered the GT350 for Owen, and when it was supplied, Owen presented it in Essex Wire livery, with a wide black stripe bordered by two thin orange stripes. The original sales invoice was in Scott's name, and he shared driving duties with Owen in its first race, the 1965 Watkins Glen 500, but Owen owned the car. (*Courtesy SAAC*)

SFM5R102 was sold to Bob Johnson, a prolific sports car driver who, having raced Corvettes for several years, switched to Cobras in 1963. He drove a Cobra Daytona Coupe in a handful of World Championship endurance races for Shelby American in 1965, including Le Mans. He was top B/Production point-scorer in SCCA Division 3 in 1965, and finished second to Jerry Titus at the 1965 ARRC at Daytona in his GT350. *(Courtesy SAAC)*

Randy Blessing purchased SFM5R103 for Walt Hane to drive. The car was supplied in June 1965. Hane's car sported Le Mans stripes, but to set it apart from the other GT350s, the sides of the roof were painted red. This very early photo captures the car prior to the red additions. Hane finished third in SCCA Division 2, and placed fourth at the 1965 ARRC at Daytona. The CFRT lettering on the front fenders stood for Central Florida Racing Team. *(Courtesy Walt Hane/Brad Leach)*

SFM5R105 was purchased by Malcolm Starr for Mark Donohue to race. This car played an important role in Donohue's transition from amateur to semi-professional driver, as he also arranged sponsorship (from Archway Ford) and assembled a small team to run the car. Through Allen Abramson, owner of Archway Ford, Donohue was selected for Ford's parts assistance program, which provided replacement parts at no charge. Donohue didn't like the way the R-model handled; he considered it too softly sprung, so began trialling different shocks and springs. He was close friends with Walt Hansgen, and asked Hansgen to share the GT350 with him at the Watkins Glen 500, in August. Hansgen had a Firestone tire deal, and Donohue decided the car would perform better with larger rear wheels and tires. Therefore, he ordered a pair of 8.5in wide American Racing 'Standards,' normally used for drag racing, and then wrapped them in the largest tire he could find in Hansgen's workshop. The pair won their class at Watkins Glen, and finished third outright, while Donohue also went on to win SCCA B/Production Division 1. Pictured is the car prior to most of Donohue's changes. *(Courtesy SAAC)*

Opposite: Zolder, Belgium. Under the guise of Ford International, three Mustangs entered the Zolder round of the 1965 European Touring Car Championship. Car 71 was driven by Lucien Bianchi, car 61 by Roy Pierpoint, and car 81 by Jacky Ickx. Pierpoint raced the same car to win the 1965 British Saloon Car Championship. This was DPK 6B, which placed second in the 1964 Tour de France, run by Alan Mann Racing. The Ickx Mustang, carrying registration ABP 325B, was an Alan Mann-built car, owned by Ford Belgium. The Bianchi Mustang had also been built by Alan Mann Racing, and owned by Gawaine Baillie, who'd raced it in the 1965 BSCC. All three Mustangs were supplied factory red, but changed to white with blue stripes partway through 1965. *(Courtesy Revs Institute, Jean Charles Martha)*

Silverstone, England. Moments after the start to the 1965 Silverstone Grand Prix Saloon Car support race, and the Mustangs of Mike Salmon, Roy Pierpoint, and Gawaine Baillie leapt ahead. Salmon's dark blue car was the former Alan Mann Racing DPK 5B which contested the 1964 Tour de France. Although Pierpoint owned his own Mustang, for this non-championship race he was aboard the Alan Brown Racing-owned car driven throughout 1965 by Jack Brabham. Brabham was competing in the Formula 1 race at this event. This was the former DPK 7B Alan Mann Racing Mustang which won the 1964 Tour de France before being sent temporarily to the United States and Canada. Baillie won this race, with Salmon finishing second. *(Courtesy Revs Institute, Albert R Bochroch)*

New Zealand. The first road racing Mustang in New Zealand was this car, owned by Ivan Segedin. It was a K-code notchback built to FIA Group 2 specification, utilizing components supplied by Shelby American. It was fitted with a Cobra competition intake manifold and four Weber carburettors.

(Courtesy Chris Swan)

The 1965 ARRC at Daytona had a combined grid of A/Production and B/Production cars, all competing for their own championships. Fastest of the B/Production cars, and qualifying second outright behind Shelby American driver Hal Keck's A/Production Cobra (number 11), was Mark Donohue in SFM5R105. Following a towing accident that required repairs and new paint, Donohue decided to reverse the GT350s colors, painting the car blue with white stripes. His mechanic George Clark fitted a set of Dickie DiBiasse cylinder heads, and Donohue was comfortably faster than Titus in the Shelby American entry. During practice, Donohue could hear the big outside rear tire rubbing against the spring leaves from the high loads around the Daytona banking, so the team fitted a spacer and ground away some of the spring metal. But it wasn't enough. During the race, while leading the B/Production class, the tire blew, putting Donohue out. Titus, running second at the time, inherited the lead, and the race win, to become 1965 SCCA ARRC B/Production National Champion. *(Courtesy SAAC)*

1966

1966 was a big year for the SCCA. In addition to a new international race series for unlimited Group 7 sports cars (Can-Am), it spread its wings further still, into sedan racing!

As part of a multi-year restructure beginning in 1961, the SCCA Board of Governors gave approval to begin hosting professional racing. John Bishop headed the project, which was not universally embraced within the SCCA. There was still a strong belief among many members that it should remain a strictly amateur club, but the SCCA needed to change with the times to protect its very survival.

Throughout the late 1950s, track promoters began urging the SCCA to start hosting professional events, and, when it refused, the tracks gradually shifted across to rival sanctioning group United States Auto Club (USAC). Now, the SCCA decided it wanted to wrestle the track promoters back again. It took until 1965 to fully repair the damage, the Times Grand Prix at Riverside being the last event recaptured by the SCCA. As part of the restructure, great care was taken to keep the amateur and professional racing separate.

The SCCA employed FIA Group 2 Touring Car regulations for its new sedan category. The European Touring Car Championship, British Saloon Car Championship, numerous European national championships, and Australian Touring Car Championship, were among those already using FIA Group 2 regulations.

For Bishop, adopting Group 2 was an easy decision. However, careful application of the rules would be needed to avoid further strain within the SCCA ranks. Group 2 regulations were incredibly detailed, and each make and model of car was required to undergo an application process for homologation with the FIA. Each vehicle had its own FIA Homologation Sheet, a comprehensive multi-page document that specified everything from individual factory part numbers, to wheel widths, minimum racing weight, right through to aftermarket parts the manufacturer wanted included as part of the process. In addition, a minimum 1000 cars must have been produced in a 12-month period.

To homologate the Mustang notchback as a Group 2 car to contest the 1966 SCCA Trans-Am Championship, Ford requested Shelby American fill out the FIA paperwork. The job was tasked to Chuck Cantwell. As Shelby American didn't have a suitable car at its LAX plant, Cantwell sent a photographer to a local Ford dealer which had a white 289-powered notchback on its lot, and photos were taken showing the car from various angles for the homologation papers. Cantwell sent the paperwork to Dearborn for final approval, but before being submitted, he requested Ford's graphics people draw some mag wheels onto the photos, as he wanted the cars to use the same magnesium American Racing wheels as used on the Shelby GT350s. The Mustang at the dealership was fitted with standard steel wheels. Those artistic efforts can be seen in the FIA's official homologation sheets.

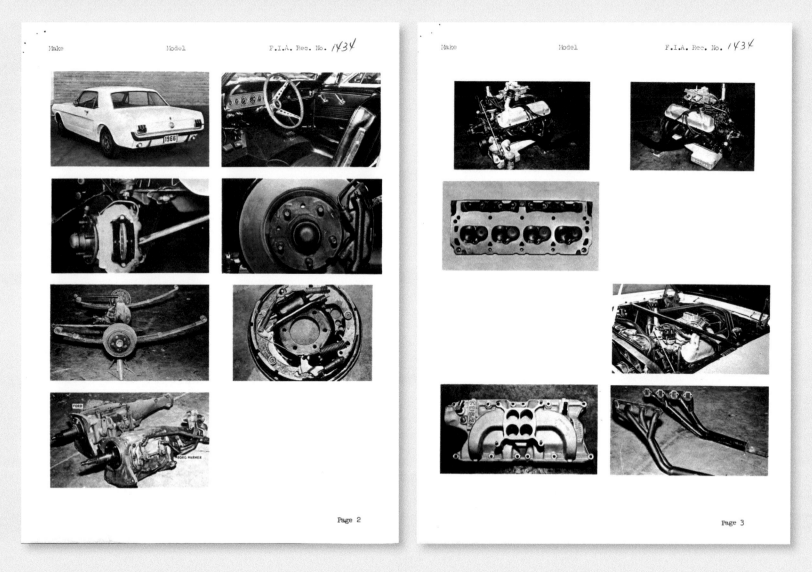

In both the British Saloon Car Championship and Australian Touring Car Championship, grids combined a broad range of cars, from tiny BMC Minis right through to massive 7-liter Ford Galaxies and Chevrolet Impalas. It was here the SCCA became more selective in its Group 2 adoption process. Fearing its grids would get infiltrated by fender-banging NASCAR stock car teams, the SCCA instigated a maximum 5000cc engine size, and 116-in wheelbase, specifically to keep these cars out.

The Galaxies competing in Great Britain and Australia were raced by sporty-car teams, such as the John Willment Group and Alan Brown Racing, who were just as adept at running spindly Formula 1 or sports cars as they were lumbering sedans. They employed open wheeler and sports car racing stars such as Dan Gurney, Jack Brabham, Graham Hill, and Denny Hulme to drive their Galaxies. There was no fender-banging, and no trouble. It was all quite orderly, but the SCCA wasn't convinced the same would apply in its own backyard. Also, it wanted to steer its new category towards attracting compact sporty sedans like the new Ford Mustang. Already, due to the runaway sales success of the Mustang, other manufacturers were well advanced in bringing their own variants to market, and the SCCA wanted to be there to capitalize.

The SCCA would split its new sedan category into four different classes, based on engine size, and using a lettering system much like its sports car racing groups to differentiate each. The classes were as follows:

A/Sedan: 2001cc-5000cc
B/Sedan: 1300cc-2000cc
C/Sedan: 1001cc-1300cc
D/Sedan: 0-1000cc

Each of the SCCA divisions would have their own multi-race regional championships.

More importantly, the SCCA would expand on its adoption of Group 2 and launch a professional road racing sedan championship, contested across

seven races, and spanning the full breadth of the country, from Sebring in Florida, to Riverside in California. Fittingly, it was called the Trans-American Sedan Championship. It was a grand name, certainly, but most people soon embraced a simplified alternative: the Trans-Am Championship.

Unlike its regional counterpart, the SCCA split the Trans-Am into just two classes:
U2: 0-2000cc
O2: 2001cc-5000cc

Both Over-2 and Under-2 would compete in the same races, but only class points would be awarded. Furthermore, there would be no Drivers' Championship, only a Manufacturers' Championship. The points-paying system was similar to that of the new Can-Am series (and Formula 1, for that matter): 9-6-4-3-2-1. Points would be awarded only to the first car representing each manufacturer to cross the finish line. Therefore, if Ford Mustangs placed first through fifth, and a Dodge Dart was sixth, Ford would score 9 points, Dodge would score 1 point.

Race distances would be a minimum of 250 miles, requiring most teams to use two drivers for each car. The Trans-Am Championship was listed on the FIA international racing calendar. The prize purse was modest.

Ford wanted representation in the inaugural Trans-Am series, and it wanted to win the Manufacturers' Championship, but its commitment was nowhere near the multimillion-dollar sledgehammer approach it applied to other racing disciplines, such as Le Mans, or NASCAR. Indeed, not only would it not provide funding for a factory race team in the Trans-Am, it requested Shelby American fill out the homologation paperwork, which it would then submit to the FIA.

Ford did, however, instruct Shelby American to construct a fleet of A/Sedan/Group 2 Mustangs to make available to customers, just to help stack the grids, and tilt the odds in its favor. Unlike the Shelby American-built Shelby GT350s, which were fitted with their own Shelby VIN tags, the Shelby

Green Valley Raceway. Having achieved its goal and won the 1965 SCCA B/Production Divisional and ARRC Nationals, Shelby had no real need to continue contesting B/Production in an official capacity in 1966. However, Carroll Shelby wanted to celebrate his team's achievements with his home crowd at Green Valley, in February 1966. So he sent a small squad to Texas, including Jerry Titus, Shelby American fabricator/race mechanic Jerry Schwarz, and 5R001. *(Courtesy Jerry Melton/etceterini.com)*

Green Valley Raceway. The plan was that Titus would win both races at Green Valley, exiting on a high-note. And everything went to script in the first race.

(Courtesy Jerry Melton/etceterini.com)

Green Valley Raceway. Gene Hamon Ford also ran a GT350 at Green Valley. This was SFM5R108. Its regular driver was Bill Steele. However, late on Saturday during the two-day event, Mexican Formula 1 racer Pedro Rodríguez was asked to drive 5R108 in the two races on Sunday. Rodríguez duly chased Titus home in the first race. He then leapt ahead of Titus at the start of the feature, and although the Shelby American driver surged back in front before the end of lap one, Rodríguez retook the lead on lap three, and held it to the end. Carroll Shelby was not impressed, and let Jerry Titus and Jerry Schwarz know his thoughts when next they gathered back at work.

(Courtesy Jerry Melton/etceterini.com)

American-built Group 2 Mustangs retained only their Ford VINs. Because the fastback Shelby GT350 was being represented in SCCA B/Production sports car racing, the notchback was chosen for sedan racing.

Most of the mechanical upgrades featured on the Shelby GT350 R-model were eligible for the Group 2 Mustang notchback. Group 2 regulations demanded the bodywork remain completely stock, although front and rear bumpers could be removed. Cars also had to retain their interior trim, but a race seat for the driver could replace the factory seat, and they could also be equipped with a roll cage. The stock steel hood had to stay. The fiberglass Shelby GT350 hood couldn't be used, and nor could the center scoop, but under the surface, most of the Shelby GT350 components could be bolted straight into a Group 2 Mustang. This was handy for Shelby American when building customer cars. These same components were sold through the Shelby American parts catalogue for

Sebring. The very first SCCA Trans-Am race was contested on March 25, 1966, as a supporter to the annual 12 Hours of Sebring. Three Mustangs were entered in the 4-hour race, the fastest of which was that driven by A J Foyt. Starting positions were determined by engine displacement. Foyt led the first half of the race until his Mustang broke.

(Courtesy William A Jordan)

those who wanted to build their own Group 2 Mustangs for Trans-Am and A/Sedan regional competition.

Having won the 1965 SCCA B/Production Nationals with the Shelby GT350, Shelby American would sit-out 1966 as an entrant. There were now numerous Shelby GT350s competing in private hands throughout the country, and indeed, GT350 racers Walt Hane and Freddy Van Beuren would finish first and third in B/Production at the 1966 ARRC.

The Mustang's main O2 class competition in the 1966 Trans-Am Championship were the Plymouth Barracudas and Dodge Darts, which actually took points away from one another, given they were being represented as two different manufacturers. In truth, Chrysler didn't care about the Trans-Am in 1966, but it was costing so little to be involved in the new series, it provided modest support to a couple of teams anyway. These were Chrysler employee Scott Harvey's Team Starfish, and Bob Tullius' Group 44.

With six of the seven rounds completed, Ford had scored three race victories (two by Tom Yeager/Bob Johnson and one by John McComb/Brad Brooker) to the two of Dodge and one of Plymouth. However, Ford and Plymouth were tied on 37 points in the Manufacturers' Championship. Therefore, Ford instructed Shelby American to commission one of its as-yet unsold customer cars, and contest the final race at Riverside. Jerry Titus was the driver. He took pole position and won the race, and Ford won the very first Trans-Am O2 Championship.

1966 Shelby GT350 production focused purely on road cars. There was no longer a requirement to build race cars, and race car demand had all but dried up. Indeed, the 1966-model road cars became a little softer, and began a gradual shift away from the hard edges of the 1965 model. Customers could now option a color combination other than Wimbledon White with Guardsman Blue stripes, a back seat, and even an automatic transmission. Racers continued using their 1965 models, although one new feature from the 1966 cars did make it across to the race cars; Pete Brock's rear brake scoops, which were now standard on the 1966 road cars.

In Australia, Ian Geoghegan won the 1966 Australian Touring Car Championship, held at Bathurst, in New South Wales. He engaged in a race-long battle with 1965 champion, Norm Beechey, who'd now switched to a 327in[3] Chevy II. The big Chevy was forced to use drum brakes in all four corners, and these eventually overheated.

For 1966, the British Saloon Car Championship switched from FIA Group 2 to the more liberal Group 5 regulations. Jack Brabham won the opening race of the championship in his Alan Brown-run Mustang, but his was to be the only Mustang victory all year. The eight-race series was dominated for the most-part by a fleet of Ford Falcon Sprints. These were left-over Alan Mann Racing cars from the 1964 Monte Carlo Rally. Because the Falcon Sprint had been homologated with a 980kg (2160lb) minimum racing weight, and fitted with fiberglass body panels, when converted to Group 5 regulations, as well as wide magnesium wheels, these cars were extremely fast, as was the Lotus Cortina run by Colin Chapman's Team Lotus, and driven by the brilliant Jim Clark. Between the Falcon Sprints, Lotus Cortinas, and Mustang, Ford clean-swept every race in the 1966 BSCC.

Sebring. The number 1 Mustang was that driven by Dick Thompson in the Sebring 4-Hour. It failed to finish. *(Courtesy William A Jordan)*

Sebring. The number 5 Mustang competing at the Sebring 4-Hour Trans-Am was driven by Ed Diamond. It too failed to finish. *(Courtesy William A Jordan)*

The first Trans-Am race may not have set the motorsport world alight, but it did make the cover of *Autosport* magazine.

Green Valley Raceway. This is SFM5R210, being driven at Green Valley by Brad Brooker. Brooker finished first in SCCA Division 4 in 1966, and placed seventh at the 1966 ARRC. *(Courtesy Jerry Melton)*

In early 1966, Tom Yeager sold Shelby GT350 SFM5R094 and debuted this Group 2 Mustang in the second round of the Trans-Am Championship. Yeager shared the car with Bob Johnson, and the pair won on debut. This was the first Trans-Am victory for Mustang. Yeager and Johnson also won at Virginia International Raceway. *(Courtesy Curtis Ross Wheatley)*

Shelby American built a small batch of race-ready Group 2 Mustangs to be sold to independents. Russell Norburn and Pete Feistman raced one such example in a selection of 1966 Trans-Am races. Their best result was second at Virginia International Raceway. All the Shelby American Group 2 Mustangs were supplied with Wimbledon White paint. This car was soon repainted red with a white stripe. *(Courtesy SAAC)*

Mark Donohue ran a limited schedule in the Malcolm Starr Shelby GT350 in 1966. Like many competitors with 1965 R-models, Donohue fitted his car with the rear brake scoops which were standard on 1966 Shelby Mustangs. *(Courtesy SAAC)*

Circuit Mont-Tremblant. Comstock Racing was, in essence, an unofficial Ford factory team, and raced several prominent Ford products during the 1960s. Here, the team transporter arrives for the Labatt 50 event with Shelby GT350 SFM5R096 (driven by Craig Fisher), and a Cobra for George Eaton. (Courtesy Denis Giguere)

Levin, New Zealand. Shelby American built and sold race-ready Group 2 Mustang notchbacks to customers all over the country, and to customers all over the world. This car was purchased by New Zealand driver Paul Fahey. Note its front fenders have been radiused out, and that its sporting a hood scoop. (Courtesy Steve Twist)

Circuit Mont-Tremblant. One of the support classes to the 1966 Can-Am Championship race at Circuit Mont-Tremblant, was a mixed collection of sedans and stock cars. Pictured leading the Chevelle of Marius Amiot and Craig Fisher's 1957 Chevrolet is John Fisher's Comstock Racing Mustang. (*Courtesy Yves St-Jean*)

Australia. Pictured at Lakeside Raceway in Queensland is Ian Geoghegan with his 1965 Mustang, being chased by arch-rival Norm Beechey in a Chevy II. Beechey had won the 1965 Australian Touring Car Championship with a Mustang, but switched to the more powerful Chevy in 1966 to better tackle the growing legion of Mustangs. (*Courtesy John Stanley*)

Green Valley Raceway. Along the Green Valley straight in the rain, the John McComb/Brad Brooker Mustang chases the Team Starfish Plymouth Barracuda of Charlie Rainville/Bob Johnson. Johnson had switched to the Plymouth when Tom Yeager's budget ran dry following the Marlboro 12 Hours. *(Courtesy Jerry Melton/etceterini.com)*

Green Valley Raceway. Five Mustangs started the Green Valley 6 Hours Trans-Am race, including the Dos Caballos Racing Team entry for Freddy Van Beuren IV/Ruben Novoa. They failed to finish. *(Courtesy Jerry Melton/etceterini.com)*

Green Valley Raceway. The John McComb/Brad Brooker Mustang won the Green Valley 6 Hours Trans-Am race by six laps. This was a Shelby American-built car. *(Courtesy Jerry Melton/etceterini.com)*

RIVERSIDE TRANS-AMERICAN SEDAN CHAMPIONSHIP

OFFICIAL 50 CENT PROGRAM

SANCTIONED BY: THE SPORTS CAR CLUB OF AMERICA, INC.
CONDUCTED BY: THE CALIFORNIA SPORTS CAR CLUB REGION, SCCA
PROMOTED BY: RIVERSIDE INTERNATIONAL RACEWAY
SANCTION NUMBER: N-40-66

Riverside International Raceway. By the final 1966 Trans-Am race, Ford and Plymouth were tied on points, so Ford paid for Shelby American to help secure the Manufacturers' Championship. Shelby used an unsold Group 2 customer car, and, with Jerry Titus driving, took the victory here at Riverside.

(Courtesy Dave Friedman)

The Van Beuren family purchased SFM5R108 off Gene Hamon in 1966 for Freddy IV to race. He qualified for the ARRC, to be held at Riverside. The Shelby was towed from Texas to California by Texan SCCA volunteers Paul Cranston and Wayne Hill, for Van Beuren to race at the ARRC. This is long-time SCCA member Cranston pictured with the car during the road trip. *(Courtesy Wayne Hill)*

When Paul Cranston and Wayne Hill towed SFM5R108 from Texas to California they stopped by Shelby American. This is the LAX facility, with the office and one of the massive hangars in the background. The office building regularly served as a backdrop for Shelby American promotional photos. *(Courtesy Wayne Hill)*

Rows of new Shelby Cobras are parked at the rear of the Shelby American
LAX facility in November 1966, along with a 1965 GT350 R-model. Obscured
behind the R-model are new 1967 Shelby Mustangs.

(Courtesy Wayne Hill)

Riverside. The 1966 SCCA ARRC was held at Riverside Raceway, in late November. This view down the pit rows captures the blue Shelby American-built Group 2 Mustang of Don Pike in the foreground. Pike worked for Shelby, and raced this Mustang with various Shelby members late in 1966. Off to the right can be seen the Cobra Caravan, a Ford transporter which toured parts of the country displaying a selection of its successful 1965 race cars, including a Cobra, Cobra Daytona Coupe, GT40, and GT350. *(Courtesy Wayne Hill)*

(Left and bottom left) Riverside. Although he didn't collect enough points to finish in the top three for SCCA Division 3 (his number shows he finished fourth in Division 1; 104), Mark Donohue was able to contest the 1966 SCCA ARRC due to two Division 1 competitors not attending. The large American Racing Standard drag wheels and big tires, as well as its forward rake, are all visible here. *(Courtesy SAAC)*

Riverside. Freddy Van Beuren IV (pictured left) at the 1966 ARRC, with a friend from Mexico (centre), and Wayne Hill (right). *(Courtesy Wayne Hill)*

(Opposite) Riverside. The A/Production and B/Production cars competed in the same race at the 1966 ARRC, although the A/Production cars were set off 30 seconds ahead. Gridded on the front two rows of the B/Production grid are Walt Hane in SFM5R103 alongside Chevrolet high-performance specialist Don Yenko in the Corvette. On row two are Ron Dykes in the Doane Spencer-built Sunbeam Tiger formerly raced by Jim Adams, and Ed Tucker in the Lotus Elan. Note that Hane has fitted his car with the wide 8.5 American Racing Standard wheels pioneered by Mark Donohue the previous year. The numbering system on the doors refers to the Division and that driver's finishing position within their Division. Therefore, Hane was from Division 2, and finished in position 1 for his Division. *(Courtesy Wayne Hill)*

Riverside. Pictured is the fourth row back for the ARRC B/Production grid. The red Shelby GT350 is SFM5R099 of Dan Gerber, while alongside is Frank Search in the Corvette. Van Beuren IV can be seen behind Search. In the row ahead of this group is Mark Donohue. On lap four, after receiving a nudge by a Corvette, Gerber crashed his GT350 heavily into a concrete wall, necessitating a red flag. Gerber sustained serious injuries and his car was destroyed. When the track was cleared and the race about to be flagged off again, some of the cars wouldn't start, Donohue's included, and he'd be disqualified for receiving outside assistance. Even though the race was red-flagged, the clock kept counting down, and the original 30-minute duration was halved.

(Courtesy Wayne Hill)

Riverside. The aftermath of Dan Gerber's shunt at the 1966 SCCA ARRC. Fortunately, despite suffering multiple injuries, Gerber himself recovered. The Shelby was a total loss.

(Courtesy Dave Wiehle)

Riverside. Walt Hane leads Ron Dykes, Don Yenko, Freddy Van Beuren, Ed Tucker and the rest of the B/Production grid at the SCCA ARRC. This is almost certainly following the restart, resulting from Dan Gerber's wreck. As well as Gerber, Mark Donohue is also absent, due to his disqualification. Other than Yenko, who was disqualified post-race for jumping the restart, this was the order in which they finished.

(Courtesy Walt Hane/Brad Leach)

1967

John Surtees, driving a Lola T70, won the inaugural SCCA Can-Am Championship for unlimited Group 7 sports cars. In doing so, he amassed more than $70,000 in prize money, a colossal sum in 1966.

Bruce McLaren, who finished third in points with his latest McLaren M1B, stated in his *Autosport* magazine column 'From The Cockpit,' he'd won more money from the 6-Round Can-Am Championship, despite not winning a single race, than he had done from the last three Formula 1 seasons.

Already, the new Can-Am Championship was being celebrated as one of the greatest road racing categories on the planet. Apart from Surtees and McLaren, other star drivers to grace its grids were Dan Gurney, Phil Hill, Jackie Stewart, Mario Andretti, Graham Hill, A J Foyt, Parnelli Jones, Pedro Rodríguez, Denny Hulme, Mark Donohue, Jim Hall, Chris Amon, and countless others. And that was just for 1966. Four of the six races had enjoyed record attendances, and every race saw the existing lap record smashed.

The new Can-Am Championship had whipped up a veritable storm, and even more hype surrounded the upcoming 1967 season. By contrast, the SCCA's other new professional road racing championship, the Trans-Am, eased itself out of the blocks a little more sedately. A J Foyt and Jochen Rindt contested the opening event at Sebring, held the day before the annual 12 Hours race. Of course, Foyt was driving a Ford GT MkII in the 12 Hours, so he was there anyway, but regardless, this pairing helped give the new Trans-Am some credibility. Foyt drove a Mustang, while Rindt was the eventual race winner in an Alfa Romeo GTA. Following Sebring, the 1966 Trans-Am settled into a contest supported predominantly by amateur racers.

Ford Motor Company, however, had seen enough potential in the Trans-Am to commit funding for two factory teams in 1967, including the Mustang, and its new Lincoln-Mercury division upmarket pony car, the Cougar.

The Mercury Cougar Trans-Am initiative was launched in late 1966. Fran Hernandez, who headed Lincoln-Mercury's racing programs, ushered in Bud Moore Engineering for the role. Bud Moore was already a highly decorated team owner in the NASCAR Grand National when Hernandez coaxed him across to Lincoln-Mercury for 1964, and he continued to build on those successes. Pony car road racing was a sizeable departure from stock car racing, but Bud Moore Engineering would prove itself highly adaptable. The two Bud Moore Cougars would be driven, for the most-part, by Parnelli Jones and Ed Leslie, with a carousel of others including Dan Gurney, David Pearson, and Peter Revson also drafted in as required.

Meanwhile, Shelby American would race a pair of the latest face-lifted Mustangs. Now with a vested interest, Ford itself completed and filed the paperwork with the FIA to homologate the 1967 Mustang. In addition to its own factory team cars, Shelby American would also continue building customer Group 2 Mustangs.

The double-threat Ford/Mercury attack would be met with strong opposition in the 1967 Trans-Am from new entrant Roger Penske, who'd campaign a single Chevrolet Camaro for Mark Donohue. Officially, General Motors wasn't involved in racing, but unofficially, it was. It built and homologated a special Camaro designed specifically for the Trans-Am, called the Z-28. Whereas the A/Sedan and Trans-Am 5000cc (305in³) maximum engine size was designed to loosely meet the Mustang's 289in³ engine size, the Camaro Z-28 came at the Trans-Am from the other direction. The small block Chevrolet engine had a 4in cylinder bore as standard, to which was mated a 3in crankshaft, providing an almost-perfect 302in³. It'd take a little while for Penske to develop the Camaro into a race winner, but while the handling and brakes needed work, the Traco-built Chevy had it over the Fords from the outset.

In stock form, the 1967 Mustang was just over 2.5in wider than the 1966 model, providing a little more engine room, and a broader track. But the Shelby American-built 1967 Group 2 Mustangs were effectively an evolution of the 1966 cars, which themselves were a Group 2 sedan version of the 1965 Shelby GT350 R-model. Engines, now topped with a pair of four-barrel

Daytona. The 1967 Trans-Am Championship kicked off at Daytona Speedway, with a 300-mile contest held the day before the annual 24 Hours race. Suddenly, the series had got a lot more serious than it had been in 1966, with factory entries from Ford, Mercury, and Chevrolet. The Bud Moore Engineering Cougars (driven by Parnelli Jones, 15, and Dan Gurney, 16) were noticeably different to the Shelby American Mustangs (Jerry Titus is in number 68), sitting much lower to the ground, and featuring full roll cages. The Cougars also rolled on steel wheels early in the season. *(Courtesy Revs Institute, Albert R Bochroch)*

Australia. Ian Geoghegan continued racing his 1965 Mustang into early 1967. The car was continuously developed, and kept getting faster. Note the neat fender flares. *(Courtesy Mike Feisst)*

Holley carburettors mounted on a new intake manifold, and with new better-breathing headers, enjoyed an increase in horsepower over 1966.

A standard Mercury Cougar was effectively a Mustang with an extra 3 inches of wheelbase, and different sheet metal and trim, but the Bud Moore Engineering Trans-Am Cougars were in total contrast to the Shelby American Mustangs. Carroll Shelby came from a sports car background, and his Mustangs were, in effect, big sports cars. Bud Moore, however, came from a stock car background, and his Cougars were more like miniature NASCAR Grand National cars. They sat very low to the ground, noses raked downwards, and were fitted with integral roll cages that provided greater rigidity and strength. In the early races, they rolled on pressed-steel wheels, but they were fast right out of the box.

Different as they were to start with, the Shelby American Mustangs and Bud Moore Engineering Cougars evolved into quite similar packages. Although fierce rivals, the two outfits appeared to be learning from each other. The Mustangs started the year still fitted with the very basic half-cage as originally fitted to 1965 Shelby GT350 R-models, but by Round 6 at Bryar were sporting a more complex full cage, like those in the Mercury. Likewise, the Bud Moore team having come from a stock car background, engaged in copious acid dipping of metal components, including entire bodyshells. The process involved submerging parts in an acid bath for a set period of time, during which the acid would eat away at the metal, considerably reducing its weight. This process was strictly illegal in the Trans-Am, but the SCCA had no real way of proving it. Shelby American debuted its first acid-dipped Mustang at Round 11 of the championship, at Stardust Raceway, Las Vegas.

Trans-Am regulations remained much the same in 1967 as they were in 1966, and still, the SCCA only held a championship for manufacturers.

Predictably, the 1967 Trans-Am Championship became a battle between the Shelby American Mustangs and Bud Moore Cougars. In the

Sebring. This is Roger West's 1965 Shelby GT350 (SFM5R538) pictured at the 1967 Sebring 12 Hours. West shared the car with Bobby Allison and Joseph Ausburn, but they failed to finish. West won the SCCA B/Production Southwest Division Championship with this car, and placed 3rd in B/Production at the 1967 SCCA American Road Race of Champions. *(Courtesy SAAC)*

end, Ford took it by two points. Mark Donohue spent the early part of the year fighting his unwieldy Camaro as the Penske team slowly bred it into a contender. He won three of the last six races, including the final two, and looked to have the momentum going into 1968.

The 1967 SCCA American Road Race of Champions was held at Daytona International Speedway, and for the third year in succession, a Shelby GT350 took the grand prize in B/Production. Freddy Van Beuren, Brad Brooker, and Roger West clean-swept the top three positions, all driving Shelby GT350s.

Ian Geoghegan won the Australian Touring Car Championship in his newly-built Mustang GTA. The car made its race debut at the ATCC event, held at Lakeside Raceway in Queensland. Norm Beechey dominated in his powerful Chevy II, but blew a tire on lap 39 of the 50-lap contest, heavily careening into a guardrail. Geoghegan, who was running second at the time, continued on unabated to take a comfortable victory.

The 1967 British Saloon Car Championship was contested over ten races, and Frank Gardner won seven of them in his Alan Mann Racing Ford Falcon Sprint. The super-lightweight Falcon Sprints maintained their dominance from 1966 under FIA Group 5 regulations. Jackie Oliver, in a Mustang, was the only driver other than Gardner to win a race. He took three victories.

Green Valley Raceway. Round 3 of the 1967 Trans-Am Championship, held at Green Valley, featured a Le Mans start, with drivers running across the track to their cars. Pole-sitter Dick Thompson in the Shelby American Mustang dropped well down the order by the time the grid got going. First away are the Mustangs of Ron Dykes and Freddy Van Beuren IV.

(All three photographs courtesy Jerry Melton/etceterini.com)

Green Valley Raceway. Jerry Titus rolled his Shelby American Mustang in practice, requiring an all-night rebuild just to make the race. He started off the rear, but was fifth by the end. Some of the damage from the rushed rebuild can still be seen here. Shelby American ran two factory Mustangs in 1967, although neither were officially entered under the Shelby American label. This car, for Titus, ran under the Terlingua Racing Team banner. Terlingua was a tiny ghost town in Southwest Texas with a surrounding 200,000 acres, purchased by Carroll Shelby and his friend David Witts. The pair planned to subdivide and sell the land, but when this came to nothing, they began hosting large parties a few times a year. They even had their own coat of arms drawn up by automotive artist, Bill Neale. Shelby decided he'd like to use the logo on his race cars, beginning in 1965. The "gawd-awful" yellow that adorned the 1967 Trans-Am car was derived from the yellow in Neale's logo. Other than at Daytona, where it still wore its Wimbledon White hue, Green Valley was the only race the Terlingua Racing Team lettering wasn't worn on the front fenders, as the team didn't have time to paint it following their all-nighter. *(Courtesy Jerry Melton/etceterini.com)*

(Left and above) Green Valley Raceway. Ron Dykes got a fast start in the Green Valley Trans-Am, but was soon chased down by the Bud Moore Cougars of Dan Gurney and Parnelli Jones, who finished first and second in that order. As it did in 1966, Shelby American built race-ready Group 2 cars for customers, the Dykes car being one of them. *(Courtesy Jerry Melton/etceterini.com)*

Green Valley Raceway. Milt Minter drove this Shelby American-built Mustang in the Trans-Am. It was owned by Clarence Mathews, and contested all but the opening race at Daytona. Minter's best result was second in Round 7 at Marlboro. Indeed, he scored several top four finishes, at a time in the series' history when it was still possible for an independent to achieve this. Here at Green Valley he was sixth. *(Courtesy Jerry Melton/etceterini.com)*

Green Valley Raceway. Bob Grossman had raced a broad range of cars, mostly sports cars, since the early 1950s, and had achieved a lot of success along the way. As well as his own cars, ranging from Porsches, Jaguars, Alfa Romeos, Ferraris ... he'd also driven for some of the most prominent sports car teams of the era, including NART and Briggs Cunningham. In 1967, he raced mostly Ford-powered products, including a Cobra, GT40, Shelby GT350, and this Shelby American-built Group 2 Mustang, entered by Dockery Ford. *(Courtesy Jerry Melton/etceterini.com)*

Green Valley Raceway. Another of the Mustangs competing in the Green Valley Trans-Am was that of Dale Wood. Note the Cragar S/S wheels and distinctive roll cage. This was an independent-built car. Wood failed to finish at Green Valley.
(Courtesy Jerry Melton/etceterini.com)

Green Valley Raceway. Freddy Van Beuren contested selected races in the 1966 Trans-Am, before switching to this car, owned by George Kirksley, but entered under Dos Caballos, in 1967. This was a Shelby-American-built car, which made its debut in Round 2 at Sebring. Shared with Paul Jett, the pair finished eighth at Green Valley.
(Courtesy Jerry Melton/etceterini.com)

Green Valley Raceway. When Bud Moore Engineering entered the Trans-Am series in 1967, it was formidably armed, hiring, among others, Dan Gurney and Parnelli Jones as drivers. *(Courtesy Jerry Melton/etceterini.com)*

Australia. Having destroyed his first Mustang in late 1965, Bob Jane eventually debuted a new car in early 1967. Jane's efforts to win the 1967 Australian Touring Car Championship ended early, when the car jammed in second gear on lap two. *(Courtesy Bruce Wells)*

racing
MAGAZINE

LIME ROCK

TRANS-AMERICAN SEDAN RACE · MAY 30   ONE DOLLAR

Australia. Ian Geoghegan raced his 1965 Mustang in the early part of 1967, before debuting this car at the 1967 Australian Touring Car Championship, held at Lakeside Raceway in Queensland. Geoghegan qualified second to Norm Beechey, in his now very fast Chevy II. Beechey extended a comfortable lead before a rear tire blew and he went careening into the Armco. Geoghegan, running second at the time, cruised to the title. *(Courtesy John Stanley)*

Lakeside, Australia. Mid-pack battle at the 1967 Australian Touring Car Championship race at Lakeside. This is New Zealand driver Rod Coppins in the ex-Geoghegan Mustang that won the 1966 ATCC. Behind is fellow Kiwi Paul Fahey in his Shelby American Mustang. Coppins finished seventh, while Fahey retired. The Lotus Cortina and BMC Mini Cooper are those of Brian Michelmore and John French. *(Courtesy John Stanley)*

Bryar. At rest in the Bryar pits. The second Shelby American factory Mustang was painted white with a red stripe down the center. Both cars had a satin black hood to prevent glare from the sun. This car was entered and sponsored by Grady Davis of Gulf Oil, and driven by Dr Dick Thompson.

(Courtesy Ron Lathrop)

Bryar. The Terlingua Racing Team Mustang of Jerry Titus rests on its stands prior to the Bryar race. Bryar was Round 6 of the 1967 Trans-Am Championship, and the Shelby American Mustangs now sported full roll cages, inspired, no doubt, by those in the Bud Moore Cougars.

(Courtesy Ron Lathrop)

Bryar. Dick Thompson is chased by Ed Leslie in the Bud Moore Cougar at Bryar. The dry track suggests this was practice day, as race day was drenched in rain.

(Courtesy Bill Sutton)

Bryar. Heading around on the pace lap, just prior to the start of the Bryar Trans-Am. On the front row are Peter Revson and Jerry Titus, followed by Ed Leslie and Milt Minter. The busy little Bryar course was better suited to the small cars. It was here in 1966 that a U2 car won a Trans-Am race outright for the second and final time, when Allan Moffat drove his Lotus Cortina to victory.

(Courtesy Ron Lathrop)

Bryar. Mark Donohue and Ed Leslie slither past the stricken Jerry Titus Mustang. Titus was hit hard by the Mustang of Ken Duclos on lap 44, sending it spiralling into the outside dirt bank, spinning multiple times before coming to rest on the infield. Titus whacked his head on the roll cage and was knocked unconscious for around 30 seconds.
(Courtesy Bill Sutton)

Circuit Mont-Tremblant. The two Dockery Ford team Mustangs of Bob Grossman (number 21) and Phil Groggins are parked outside the Grey Rock Inn, for the 4 Hour race at Circuit Mont-Tremblant. Although not a Trans-Am championship race, the event paid $25,000 in prize money, ensuring it attracted a sizeable grid. Grossman finished seventh, while Groggins didn't get a start, after wrecking his Mustang in practice. (Courtesy Denis Giguere)

Circuit Mont-Tremblant. Bob West (number 15) and Bob Johnson hard at work during the four-hour race at Circuit Mont-Tremblant. Ultimately, neither finished, although West did lead for a time after qualifying third. Johnson's car was believed to have served as an engineering prototype at Kar-Kraft. He didn't own it, Ford/Kar-Kraft did. Note the wheels on this car. These are also believed to have been designed and manufactured by/for Kar-Kraft. (Courtesy Denis Giguere)

Marlboro. Outside the Goodyear trailer and deep in discussion is Jerry Titus, wearing the race suit. To his right is Shelby American Project Manager Chuck Cantwell. Cantwell was himself a highly accomplished racer, and although he quit racing when he joined Shelby American, he still jumped at the chance to compete when he could. (Courtesy Don Struke)

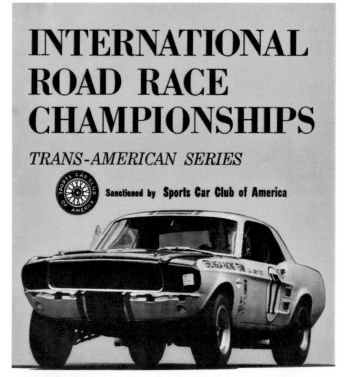

Marlboro. The Shelby American Mustang of Jerry Titus prior to the start of the Marlboro 300 Trans-Am. This was the first time the Trans-Am held separate races for U2 and O2 cars, with each car required to have two drivers. Titus and Bert Everett shared Everett's Porsche in the U2 race, held on the Saturday, while in the Sunday O2 race, Jim Adams joined him in the Mustang. *(Courtesy Don Struke)*

Marlboro. Pace lap for the Marlboro O2 Trans-Am race, with the Mark Donohue/Craig Fisher Penske Camaro alongside the Ed Leslie/Peter Revson Bud Moore Cougar. Following are the Titus/Adams and Thompson/Ed Lowther Shelby Mustangs, Pete Feistmann/Russ Norburn Mustang, and Cale Yarborough/Lee Roy Yarbrough Cougar. Donohue and Fisher raced the Camaro to its very first Trans-Am victory, followed by the Minter/Allan Moffat Mustang, and Titus/Adams Mustang. *(Courtesy Revs Institute, Duke Q Manor)*

(Opposite) Brands Hatch, England. In 1966, the British Saloon Car Championship switched to the liberal FIA Group 5 regulations, allowing the super-lightweight Falcon Sprints to dominate. The only non-Falcon driver to win in 1967 was Jackie Oliver in the Mustang seen here leading the pack. Oliver took two victories during the ten-race series, including here at Brands Hatch, Round 8. In the background, among the busy pack heading down the Brands Hatch hill, is Australian driver Bryan Thomson, who raced in Britain during 1967 with the ex-Norm Beechey Mustang. *(Courtesy Mike Hayward)*

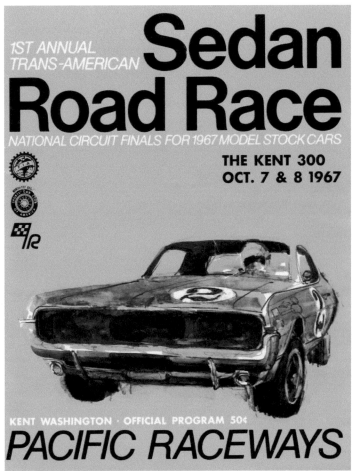

Levin, New Zealand. Shelby American built and sold 1967 Group 2 Mustangs for customers all over the world, including New Zealand racer Norm Barry, who raced under the pseudonym Frank Bryan, which was actually his two middle names. This car raced in New Zealand with a quartet of Weber carburettors, rather than the pair of four-barrel Holleys it was supplied with. *(Courtesy Steve Twist)*

Levin, New Zealand. New Zealand racer Rod Coppins purchased the Mustang raced by Ian Geoghegan from 1965 through early 1967, and which won the 1966 Australian Touring Car Championship. Coppins didn't enjoy nearly the level of success Geoghegan did with the car. *(Courtesy Steve Twist)*

Levin, New Zealand. Paul Fahey had the fastest racing sedan in New Zealand in 1967. His was a 1966 Shelby American-built Group 2 car which he'd continued to develop. New Zealand used FIA Group 5 regulations, and most of the Kiwi Mustangs were fitted with Cobra intake manifolds and quad-Weber carburettors. *(Courtesy Steve Twist)*

1968

By 1968, the dynamic between Ford Motor Company and Shelby American had changed. Despite a partnership that had proven beneficial for both parties, Ford began increasingly to wrestle control of both the road and race car programs previously entrusted to Shelby.

From late 1967, Ford moved Shelby Mustang road car production closer to its head office, in Michigan, resulting in the shut-down of the LAX facility. Furthermore, Ford had specialty engineering company Kar-Kraft build the 1968 Trans-Am Mustang chassis, a job previously performed by Shelby American.

In late 1967, just prior to the road car production operation moving from Los Angeles to Michigan, two new companies were formed, including the Shelby Parts Company, and Shelby Racing Company, both of which operated under the parent company Shelby American. The race team and parts company moved to a new, much smaller facility, in Torrance.

Ford decided it didn't want a repeat of the 1967 Trans-Am Championship, in which two of its brands were pitted against one another, squabbling over race victories. It instead opted to reduce its effort to a single team.

NASCAR president Bill France was in the throes of establishing his own version of the Trans-Am series, with races contested strictly on speedway ovals of varying lengths, layouts, and surfaces. The success of the Trans-Am and of the pony car market had prompted much interest in pony car racing, both from manufacturers and race fans, and France wanted a chunk of the pie. His new series was named NASCAR Grand Touring, and it kicked off in 1968. With Ford support, Bud Moore took his Cougars across to the inaugural NASCAR Grand Touring Championship.

Ford Special Vehicles first enlisted Kar-Kraft for its sizable Ford GT40 sports car racing assault on the Le Mans 24 Hours race. That program concluded at the end of 1967, resulting in two victories at La Sarthe in 1966 and 1967, and successive racing evolutions on the GT40. By now, Fran

Daytona. In 1968, the rapid rise of the Trans-Am series was telling in its induction as a stand-alone class at the 1968 Daytona 24 Hours. 24 Trans-Am cars started the race, where they shared track space with the Sports Prototypes and GT cars. Trans-Am points were awarded based on finishing positions relating to other Trans-Am cars, not outright positions. Sam Posey and Jim Kauffman drove the Clarence Mathews-owned Mustang to 21st outright and fifth in Trans-Am O2. *(Courtesy Jim McGhee)*

Hernandez was overseeing the entire Ford racing operation, and even had his office based at Kar-Kraft.

At the start of 1967, Trans-Am cars were essentially modified road cars, but such was their rate of development that by 1968 they'd evolved into pure-bred racers. To that end, Hernandez had Kar-Kraft pour its immense engineering resources into designing and building the 1968 factory Trans-Am

Daytona. The two Shelby Racing Co Mustangs that contested the 1968 Daytona 24 Hours were actually 1967 cars rebuilt by Kar-Kraft. Jerry Titus/Ronnie Bucknum shared the number 1 car, with Horst Kwech/Allan Moffat in number 2. Through a combination of speed, reliability, and clever pit-work, Titus/Bucknum finished fourth outright, and first in Trans-Am, headed only by a trio of Porsche 907 Prototypes. *(Courtesy Fran Hernandez)*

Mustangs. The operation was overseen by Kar-Kraft engineer Lee Dykstra. It wasn't a popular decision at Shelby Racing Company, but the Kar-Kraft Mustangs were an engineering marvel.

Outwardly, the 1968 factory Mustang Trans-Am racers didn't appear a whole lot different to their 1967 counterparts. Clearly, the 1968 models sat lower to the ground, and their 15x8in magnesium American Racing Torq Thrust wheels and massive Goodyear Bluestreak racing tires sheltered beneath much broader fender flares. But beneath the skin, they couldn't have been more contrasting. Indeed, the 1967 Shelby American Trans-Am

Mustangs had more in common with the 1965 Shelby GT350 R-model than they did the 1968 Kar-Kraft Mustangs. Furthermore, the 1968 Kar-Kraft Mustangs had more in common with the 1969-1971 factory Mustangs that were to follow than they did the 1967 Shelby American Mustangs. That was the level at which Kar-Kraft operated.

Much emphasis went into suspension design, with the front suspension components virtually all scratch-built or heavily modified, including upper and lower control arms, spindles, hubs, center links, idler arm, ball joints and sway bar. The front strut rods were designed to accept a bearing rather

Daytona. The Bob Grossman/Bob Dini 1967 Mustang finished Daytona 23rd outright and 6th in Trans-Am O2. *(Courtesy Jim McGhee)*

than the standard rubber bushings. Virtually nothing was stock. The rear suspension featured a pair of over-rider bars mounted on top of the axle and running forward attaching to the chassis rails, with Watts-link and sway bar. Spherical bearings connected the front spring eyes, with rubber bushes in the rear. Although not a true four-link design, by using spherical bearings to mount the front of the leaves, and working in conjunction with the two over-rider bars running parallel above, the front half of the leaves played the role of the lower two links of a four-link design. In addition, the leaves themselves were narrower than stock to allow more tire clearance. The axles were fully-floating, and Koni shocks were utilized front and rear.

Bodyshells were acid-dipped. Kar-Kraft then welded the seams, and the sophisticated roll cage design markedly increased chassis rigidity, while at the same time, great attention was paid to weight reduction wherever possible. There was extensive hole-sawing through any non-structural metal sections that could be covered up with trim pieces, and hidden from SCCA technical inspectors. Such actions were illegal, as was acid dipping and the use of thin-gauge body panels, but all featured on the Kar-Kraft Mustangs. Owens-Corning Fibreglass produced special thin window glass. Nothing was overlooked.

The first two 1968 cars delivered to Shelby Racing Co from Kar-Kraft were actually two of its 1967 cars, comprehensively rebuilt, and given 1968 VINs.

The SCCA made some small amendments to the Trans-Am O2 regulations for 1968, drifting away slightly from adhering fully to the FIA Group 2 rules. Firstly, fender flaring was now legal, provided the side-profile remained unchanged. Also, it dropped the FIA Group 2 minimum weights that differed for each car in favor of a minimum 2800lb rule which applied to all Trans-Am O2 cars. Likewise, it set the maximum wheel width for O2 cars at 8in. Tires were free.

SCCA regulations allowed any brakes to be utilized, but they had to be sourced from a mass-produced vehicle built by the same parent company.

Therefore, the 1968 factory Mustangs used larger Lincoln brake rotors and calipers up front. Lincoln has a different stud pattern to Ford – 5x5 (5x127) versus 5x4.5 (5x114.3) for the Ford – requiring wheels with different stud patterns be used front to rear.

For 1968, Ford also decided it needed to bridge the horsepower gap to the Chevy teams. Its solution was the tunnel-port 302. This was a new cylinder head design, featuring large intake ports that took a more direct route from the intake manifold to the cylinders, rather than curving around the pushrod holes. The pushrods themselves were housed in their own tunnels that ran straight through the intake ports. The design had already proven successful in Ford's big block NASCAR stock car program, but the concept didn't translate at all well to small block road racing engines.

Due to the layout of oval speedway tracks, NASCAR stock car engines remain in a near-constant high rev range, feeding huge gulps of air through the big intake ports to the cylinders. However, with a small 302in³ engine, run on a road course with a diverse range of corners and corner speeds, the tunnel-port engines suffered from poor throttle response in the lower rev range. To make power, they needed to breathe; they needed to be revved hard, up around 9000rpm, but in doing so, would literally shake themselves to pieces. Plus, the high revolutions prevented oil from circulating around the engine as it needed to, resulting in seizures.

Shelby Racing Co engine builder John Dunn worked to find a solution before the first race of the 1968 Trans-Am Championship, as did Ford's engine division and Kar-Kraft. The opening Trans-Am race was held at Daytona, as part of the annual 24 Hours race. Although sharing track space with the prototypes, GTs, and other classes, Trans-Am points would be awarded only to finishing positions in relation to other Trans-Am cars. Impressively, the number 1 Shelby Racing Co Mustang's tunnel-port engine held together for the entire 24 hours. Even more impressive was that the car finished fourth outright, behind a trio of Porsche Works Team 907 prototypes. Jerry Titus and

Ronnie Bucknum shared the driving duties, while Horst Kwech and Allan Moffat drove the second car, which retired with suspension failure.

The tunnel-port in the Titus/Bucknum Mustang also survived the full duration at the Sebring 12 Hours, Round 2 of the 1968 Trans-Am, although the Shelby Racing Co team was upstaged by the two Penske Racing Camaros of Mark Donohue/Craig Fisher, and Joe Welch/Bob Johnson, which finished third and fourth outright, behind two factory Porsche 907s. Titus/Bucknum were fifth outright, third in Trans-Am.

The remaining 11 races were of much shorter duration, but curiously, it was here the tunnel-port engines became increasingly troublesome. Titus blew his tunnel-port to pieces in Round 3, at War Bonnet, although his team-mate for the weekend, Parnelli Jones, managed to keep his together. Jones qualified second fastest and finished third after an unscheduled stop to have part of the throttle-linkage rebuilt. He finished third, but had been fast enough to win.

It was after the War Bonnet race Ford decided it would intervene, and build the engines in-house. Up to this point, Shelby Racing Co had built its own engines. From Round 4, at Lime Rock, the problems intensified, and engine failures increased. More often than not, at least one car suffered a broken engine at each race event. Relations between the Shelby team and Ford soured further, as Ford insisted the Shelby crew be limited purely to engine installation and removal, nothing more, and only with a designated Ford employee present. Titus took a surprise victory in Round 10 at Watkins Glen, but in Round 11, at Continental Divide, the saga reached its lowest ebb: both cars blew an engine in Friday testing, and again on Saturday, and again in the race.

Following the Continental Divide embarrassment, Ford relented and allowed Shelby Racing Co to prepare its own engines for the last two races at Riverside and Kent. Horst Kwech drove the number 2 Mustang to an unexpected victory at Riverside, while Titus blew an engine. This was to be Titus' last race as a Shelby driver. The character-building season had

him seeking new opportunities, resulting in a partnership with Canadian entrepreneur Terry Godsall. In 1969, T/G (Titus/Godsall) Racing would run a Pontiac-funded Trans-Am program with the Firebird, but for the last 1968 race, they quickly hashed-together a Chevy Camaro fitted with Firebird sheet metal, and powered by a Z28 302, and Titus duly put it on pole. He led the first half of the race, before, ironically, the engine broke.

Shelby Racing Co didn't build any customer cars in 1968. Independent teams were left to go-it alone. In hindsight, that would prove a blessing, as they were saved the aggravation of battling the tunnel-port 302.

In Australia, the Mustang enjoyed considerably more success, with Ian Geoghegan winning his third Australian Touring Car Championship in succession, and his fourth in total. Still contested as a single-race championship, the event was staged at Warwick Farm, in New South Wales. The 34-lap, 76-mile contest attracted a thirty-car entry, which featured seven Mustangs, three of which had travelled from New Zealand. Geoghegan, racing the same GTA notchback he'd won with in 1967, fended off early challenges from the Camaro of Norm Beechey and the Mustang of Bob Jane, to eventually pull away to a comfortable victory.

Daytona. The Kwech/Moffat Mustang arrives for service. The Shelby team cars changed color every race during the early part of the season. After Daytona, powder blue wasn't used again. This car retired from the Daytona race when a spring tower failed. *(Courtesy Fran Hernandez)*

Daytona. After a long 24 hours, the Posey/Kauffman Mustang follows the Mark Konig/Tony Lanfranchi Nomad MkI Prototype across the finish line. The Mustang was classified 21st outright and fifth in Trans-Am O2. *(Courtesy Jim McGhee)*

Sebring. Kwech and Moffat again teamed up in the second Shelby Racing Co entry. They retired with engine failure. The 1968 Kar-Kraft Trans-Am Mustangs were noticeably more purposeful than their 1967 counterparts, sitting much closer to the ground and sporting broad fender flares to house the latest fat Goodyears and 8in wide wheels. As at Daytona, the two factory Mustangs at Sebring were the teams 1967 models rebuilt by Kar-Kraft. *(Courtesy Doug Morton)*

Sebring. Dos Caballos raced its 1967 Mustang in the Sebring 12 Hours, driven by Freddy Van Beuren IV/Ruben Novoa/Raul Perez Gama. The gearbox failed after just 25 laps. *(Courtesy Doug Morton)*

War Bonnet. Pictured in the pits for the War Bonnet Trans-Am is the number 2 Shelby Racing Co Mustang, driven here by Parnelli Jones, plus Malcolm Starr's Mustang, and the U2 Alfa GTA of Vic Provenzano. Starr had a big shunt in this race, ending up in the spectator area where four people were injured, necessitating the race being temporarily stopped. Jones qualified second to Mark Donohue in the Penske Camaro, and the pair battled furiously for the lead in the opening segment before Starr crashed. When the race got going once more, Parnelli briefly took the lead before pitting for new tires. His race was later delayed with a throttle-linkage problem, and he finished third. Titus, in the other Mustang, broke an engine. Following this race, Ford decided to take control of the engine-building program, which further soured an already disintegrating relationship with Shelby. *(Courtesy Forrest K Bond)*

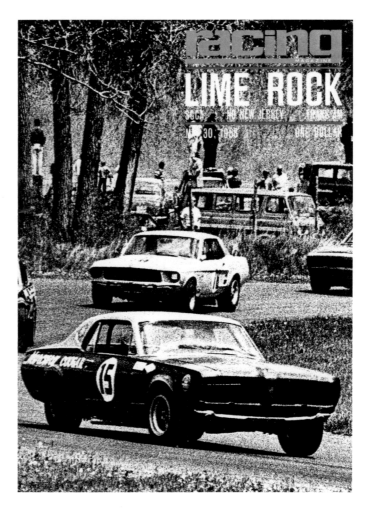

Bryar. One of the Shelby Racing Co crew works on one of the factory Mustang engines. Or maybe they had just fitted it. Engine replacements were common for the team in 1968. *(Courtesy Ron Lathrop)*

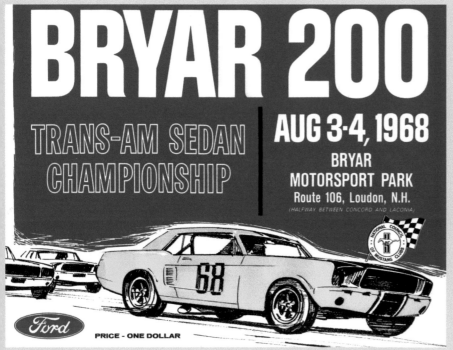

Bryar. Despite the vast sums being spent in the Trans-Am by 1968, most tracks still featured rudimentary pit facilities. Shelby Racing Co utilizes a dustbin as a work bench to store the fabricated air plenum for one of its Mustangs.

(Courtesy Ron Lathrop)

Bryar. Driver parades were a popular pre-race formality in the Trans-Am. Here, Shelby Racing Co drivers Jerry Titus and Horst Kwech take a sedate tour in the latest 1968 Shelby GT500KR convertible. *(Courtesy Bill Sutton)*

Bryar. Pace lap for the Bryar Trans-Am has the two Shelby Racing Co Mustangs of Jerry Titus (1) and Horst Kwech against Mark Donohue in the Penske Camaro, with Peter Revson's factory AMC Javelin just appearing in shot. Titus and Kwech ran 1-2 until Kwech's engine blew on lap 50. Titus spent several laps in the pits having a new differential fitted. Donohue won. *(Courtesy Bill Sutton)*

Bryar. Kwech powers his Shelby Racing Co Mustang on another lap, before engine failure halted his charge on lap 50. In the early races, the Shelby Mustangs changed color every race. From Round 7 at Circuit Mont-Tremblant, they were painted dark blue with white stripe, and remained so for the rest of the year. *(Courtesy Ron Lathrop)*

Bryar. Ford was active in promoting its products through Trans-Am races. Official Pace Car for the 1968 Bryar Trans-Am was a Shelby GT500KR convertible. George Follmer in a factory Javelin and Mark Donohue in the race-winning Camaro race by in the background. *(Courtesy Ron Lathrop)*

Bryar. Mid-pack battle, headed by Skip Barber's Camaro, chased by John McComb's Mustang. Although he raced open wheelers and sports cars predominantly, Barber, who went on to create a successful racing driver school, also contested sedan races on occasion. Here at Bryar he finished seventh, while McComb was fourth. McComb received assistance from Shelby American in late 1967 to help Ford win the Manufacturers' Championship in his independent Mustang. In 1968, he was a little disappointed not to have received a new tunnel-port 302. He eventually realised this was a blessing in disguise. *(Courtesy Bill Sutton)*

SFM6S1218 was a white 1966 Shelby GT350 Hertz rental car, damaged by fire when almost new. It was purchased by sports car racers Richard Gamboni and Clint White after their GT350 R-model SFM5R527 had been destroyed in a crash at Camp Stoneman. Parts from the wrecked R-model were transferred across to the rebuilt Hertz Shelby, which was repainted metallic green with gold stripes. The pair began racing it in late 1966.

(Courtesy SF Region Archive)

Although best known for its long and successful achievements in drag racing, as well as the creation of the Cobra-Jet Fords of the late 1960s, Tasca Ford supported this Mustang road racer, owned by Tasca Ford High-performance Sales Manager Dean Gregson. Ford Motor Company also provided some support, via factory Sales Representative, Dave Aronson. The notchback, with Gregson driving, ran SCCA A/Sedan races in 1968, in preparation for stepping up to the Trans-Am in 1969. It also played a role in developing the Boss 302 for 1969. After contesting two Trans-Am races in 1969, it was heavily damaged at Thompson Speedway, so Gregson moved the components across to a new 1969 Mustang SportsRoof. *(Courtesy Hank Fournier/Nick De Vitis)*

Australia. Ian Geoghegan won the 1968 Australian Touring Car Championship for the third time in succession. Here he is chasing the Mustang of Fred Gibson. Geoghegan's Mustang had been built in Australia by John Sheppard, using various Shelby American components. Gibson's car, which was first raced in Australia in 1967 by Greg Cusack, was a Shelby American-built customer car.

(Courtesy Oldracephotos/Simpson)

Australia. Bob Jane continued development of his 1967 Mustang throughout 1968. It sat noticeably lower than the other Australian Mustangs, and also sprouted front and rear spoilers. Jane qualified third for the 1969 Australian Touring Car Championship, behind Geoghegan and Norm Beechey's new Camaro, but his engine expired on lap nine while chasing **Beechey.** *(Courtesy Perry Drury)*

A gritty set of photos, but of great interest. In late 1968, despairing of the troubled tunnel-port 302 disaster, the Shelby team tested an engine fitted with aluminum Gurney-Weslake cylinder heads and four Weber carburettors at Riverside. A giant hole had to be cut in the hood to fit the Webers and allow them to breathe. Horst Kwech drove, and reported back his enthusiasm. Results of the test were then relayed to Fran Hernandez, at Ford, in the hope the setup could be adopted for the remaining 1968 races, and into 1969. But it hadn't been homologated for use in 1968. Furthermore, Ford opted for a cheaper package for 1969, in what would become the Boss 302. *(Courtesy Fran Hernandez)*

Watkins Glen hosted Round 10 of the 1968 Trans-Am Championship, and here, Jerry Titus chases the Penske Camaros of Mark Donohue and Sam Posey, and Peter Revson's AMC Javelin down the front straight. This time, the tunnel-port 302 in Titus' Mustang held together, and he won, from Posey and an ill Donohue. *(Courtesy Revs Institute, David Nadig)*

Pukekohe, New Zealand. Paul Fahey enjoyed another successful year in New Zealand, still aboard his Shelby American 1966 Mustang. He is seen here leading the Mustang of Red Dawson and Camaro of Spencer Black at Pukekohe. (Courtesy Steve Twist)

Levin, New Zealand. Red Dawson purchased the 1967 Shelby American-built Group 2 Mustang from Norm Barry in 1968, having struggled the previous season with the old Ivan Segedin Mustang. He was the only driver capable of regularly taking on Paul Fahey. (Courtesy Steve Twist)

Ford circulated material within the company of its various operations and programs, including its racing activities. The Trans-Am program was one of its most important by 1968, having withdrawn from Le Mans. *(Courtesy Fran Hernandez)*

TRANS-AM SEDAN MUSTANG

THE FORD TRANS-AM SERIES SEDAN IS DERIVED FROM THE BASIC MUSTANG TWO-DOOR HARDTOP. IN 1968, THE ADVANCED CONCEPTS ENGINEERING ACTIVITY PROVIDED ENGINEERING, CAR BUILD AND SUPPORT SERVICES.
THIS ENGINEERING INCLUDED COMPLETE CHASSIS, SUSPENSION, STEERING AND BRAKE DESIGN AS WELL AS BODY AERODYNAMICS AND WIND TUNNEL TESTING.

One of the very early 1969 Kar-Kraft Trans-Am Mustangs appears in this Ford internal material. Engineers are fitting the roll cage, and carrying out various chassis and bodywork modifications that would carry across the various factory team cars. Note the hole in the rear quarter for the faux brake ducts which was standard on all 1969 Mustang SportsRoofs except the Boss 302. By the time metal work was complete, this was filled in. Production 1969 Boss 302 Mustangs didn't have this hole, but none of the 1969-model factory Trans-Am Mustangs were genuine Boss 302s. *(Courtesy Fran Hernandez)*

KAR-KRAFT MERRIMAN

COMPLETE COMPETITION CARS, SUCH AS THIS TRANS-AM MUSTANG, ARE CONSTRUCTED ON A
SOUND ENGINEERING BACKGROUND OF COMPUTER ANALYSIS, DESIGN, TEST AND DEVELOPMENT.

This is the beautifully finished Kar-Kraft prototype 1969 Trans-Am Mustang (9F02R112073), pictured in December 1968. Some of the impressive detailing that went into the 1969 program can be seen in this car, including the drooped nose, the clean body lines and tucked bumpers, the broadened stamped rear fenders, and the 5x5 Lincoln front wheel studs. The focus was on getting the car right down on the ground, to make it aerodynamically efficient, and to make it rigid. The deep front spoiler was designed to limit the air flow beneath the car, to aid front downforce and prevent lift. The front spoiler was homologated through being made available on the road cars. This car was destined for Shelby Racing Company. *(Courtesy Fran Hernandez)*

1969

Following Ford's spectacular failure in the 1968 Trans-Am series, where it barely beat the brand new American Motors Javelin equip for second, efforts were ramped up for 1969.

Bud Moore was brought back to the Trans-Am following his year away racing NASCAR Grand Touring, and he'd run a multi-car Mustang team, as would Shelby Racing Company.

By 1969, the SCCA Trans-Am series had developed into one of the world's most important and influential racing categories, and manufacturer participation continued to grow year-on-year. Pontiac joined Ford, Chevrolet, and American Motors, with all running a minimum two cars per race. Only Chrysler was absent.

With more manufacturers came increased competition and pressure, prompting Ford to double-down on its fire-power. As there was no longer a Shelby GT350 sports car race program, the new-shape 1969 Mustang was homologated for Group 2 in the fastback/SportsRoof body style for the first time.

Once again, Kar-Kraft was charged with designing and building the cars that the Shelby and Moore teams would race. Kar-Kraft supplied these cars in both fully completed and partially-completed form. At least three cars were supplied in completed form; one each was sent to Shelby Racing Company and Bud Moore Engineering. Then partially-completed cars were supplied for the teams to finish themselves. Both teams were supplied with surface plates. During the course of 1969, Shelby Racing Co would receive a total of four cars, while Bud Moore received three. A further car, initially delivered incomplete to Moore's workshop, was gifted to Allan Moffat, who took it to Australia, and another car was supplied to Smokey Yunick, who'd followed his friend, Semon "Bunkie" Knudsen, from Chevrolet to Ford. Yunick's was the third completed Kar-Kraft car.

Although a face-lifted model compared to that of 1968, and carrying the new SportsRoof body style, the 1969 Kar-Kraft Mustangs were effectively an evolution of the cars built for the 1968 Trans-Am. Suspension design and build processes remained largely unchanged. Ultimately, the 1968 Kar-Kraft Mustangs were good cars let down by bad engines.

Emphasis for the 1969 Mustangs focused on aerodynamic efficiency, and having the cars hug the ground, bringing their centre of gravity as low as could be achieved. Given that all Trans-Am cars were so evenly matched in terms of horsepower, any small gains were fully exploited.

The 1969 factory Mustangs featured drooped front bodywork to aid aerodynamics, and to get the new front spoiler right down near the track surface. This, the Ford/Kar-Kraft crew termed the 'catwalk.' The catwalk involved slicing a tapered pie-cut along the inner fender sheet metal on each side just above the front spring towers, culminating in a 2in section along the front. This helped reduce frontal mass, aided aero efficiency, and, with its daisy-cutter front chin-spoiler, minimized front-end lift. The rear sections of the front fenders were massaged/extended/shortened as required to cleanly meet the doors, so as not to alert understandably suspicious SCCA technical inspectors.

Operating in a grey area just outside the rules was something all the factory teams were doing by 1969. Indeed, former racer Walt Hane, who was a tech inspector for the SCCA in 1969, could see some form of manipulation had taken place with the factory Mustangs' front bodywork. He visited local Ford dealerships and took engine compartment measurements, and then measured the Bud Moore cars. They were different, but when he questioned Bud Moore, Moore challenged Hane to show him the changes. He couldn't. Incidentally, all the factory Trans-Am Mustangs had the drooping reduced to one inch part way through the season.

The Mustang bodies, supplied from Ford without sound deadener and seam sealer, were acid-dipped, and then drastically hole-sawed in areas tech inspectors couldn't see, or that would ultimately be covered by trim pieces. Minimum weight for 1969 Trans-Am cars was 2900lb, without driver and

Bud Moore Engineering built this white (with Pepsi signage) 1969 Mustang SportsRoof for Mexican racer Moises Solana. It wasn't a Kar-Kraft car, but rather one built specifically by Bud Moore Engineering to fulfil a customer order. Starting as a six-cylinder model, it was rebuilt as a Boss 302, and delivered to Solana in April 1969. It contested its first race that same month, and won on debut. Tragically, Solana was killed in a racing accident in July 1969, after which, the Mustang was sold to Freddy Van Beuren IV, who campaigned it for several years. Solana is pictured chasing Memo Rojas in one of the earlier Shelby de Mexico team cars. Shelby de Mexico was the creation of Eduardo Velazquez, who teamed up with Carroll Shelby to import and distribute Shelby parts into Mexico. In 1967, Shelby de Mexico began converting Mexican-built Mustang GT notchbacks (the fastback shape wasn't built in Mexico) into Shelby GT350s, and supported its own factory race team. This car was shortly superseded with a 1969 Shelby de Mexico race car. *(Courtesy Bernard from Mexico)*

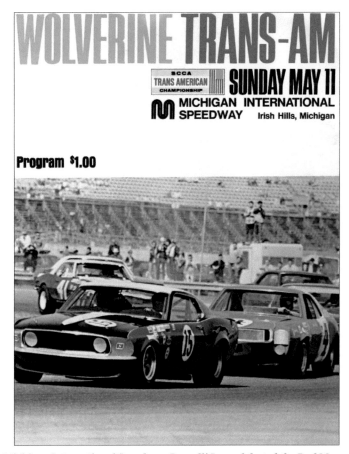

fuel. The goal was to get the Mustangs beneath the minimum weight, and then add ballast as required, to keep the centre of gravity low, but also to balance out the front-rear weight distribution. Nothing was overlooked in the quest to save weight. Even shorter window crank handles were used.

As they had done in 1968, the factory Mustangs wore larger Lincoln brake rotors and calipers in the front.

The first two 1969 Kar-Kraft Trans-Am race Mustangs left the Dearborn, Michigan, assembly plant stamped as R-code 428 big block cars, while the remaining cars were all M-code 351 small block cars. VINs for the two R-code cars, supplied late in 1968, were: 9F02R112073 and 9F02R112074. Chassis 073 went to Shelby Racing Co, and chassis 074 to Bud Moore.

The M-code cars, which were ordered from Ford in early 1969, were numbered in sequence 9F02M148623-9F02M148629. Cars 623 and 625 went to Bud Moore, cars 627-629 to Shelby Racing Co, 626 to Smokey Yunick, and 624 to Allan Moffat.

Prior to the end of the 1968 Trans-Am season, the Shelby team, with Kwech at the wheel, ran an extensive engine test at Riverside. The test

Michigan International Speedway. Parnelli Jones debuted the Bud Moore Engineering 1969 Kar-Kraft Boss 302 Mustang not at a Trans-Am race, but the NASCAR Grand Touring Daytona Citrus 250, which used the combined oval and road course layout. A photo from that race appeared on the program cover for the Wolverine Trans-Am at Michigan International Speedway.

Michigan International Speedway. Bud Moore and Parnelli Jones talk tactics. After making the odd cameo appearance in the Trans-Am since 1967, Jones became a full-time driver for Bud Moore in 1969. *(Courtesy Ron Lathrop)*

Michigan International Speedway. Peter Revson switched from the factory AMC Javelin team to Shelby Racing Co in 1969, to drive the number 1 car. He was invariably the fastest Shelby driver all year, but didn't win a race.

(Courtesy Ron Lathrop)

involved trialling an engine fitted with aluminum Gurney-Weslake cylinder heads, and a quartet of two-barrel Weber carburettors atop a special intake manifold, all supplied by Dan Gurney. Kwech enthusiastically reported the Gurney-Weslake engine to be a significant upgrade over the unloved tunnel-port, and that throttle response and driveability were all much improved. There was brief hope this option could be used for the remaining 1968 events, but as it hadn't been homologated for the Mustang, the team had to soldier on with the tunnel-port. Incidentally, Ford didn't actually build the required number of tunnel-port headed motors to make them legal, but given their abysmal record, this was quickly overlooked

The Gurney-Weslake setup was briefly considered by Ford for the 1969 Trans-Am Mustangs, but discounted due to the high costs of building the required minimum 1000 cars with this arrangement. Instead, a cross-breed combination, mating a Windsor engine block with the canted-valve cylinder heads from the new Cleveland engine, eventually gained approval. Ford built the minimum required number of cars in 1969, which was marketed as the Mustang Boss 302.

The 1969 factory Mustangs used a pair of giant Holley Dominator carburettors, ranging from 1050cfm through to 1150cfm.

Bud Moore Engineering hired Parnelli Jones and George Follmer to drive its cars, while Shelby Racing Co had Peter Revson in one car, and, for the most part, Horst Kwech in the other. Sam Posey subbed for Revson at Lime Rock, where Shelby took its only race victory of the season, while Dan Gurney drove Kwech's car twice: at Laguna Seca and Kent.

Although essentially armed with the same cars, Shelby Racing Co and Bud Moore Engineering went their separate ways regarding fitted parts and setups, and Shelby installed a couple of extra tubes in the roll cage that extended to support the cowl. Shelby used Koni shock absorbers; Bud Moore favored Gabriel.

Mustangs won four of the first five races in the 1969 Trans-Am series, and looked to storm the Manufacturers' Championship. However, a spate of wrecks at Michigan, Mid-Ohio, and Circuit Mont-Tremblant massively depleted the fleet, leaving the teams to cobble together repairs and rebuilds when they should have been developing. Furthermore, the Shelby cars were fitted with Goodyear tires, and the Bud Moore cars with Firestones. The Goodyears were the better tire in 1969, but among the Ford camp, the Bud Moore cars were faster – until they used up their tires.

Many races in 1969 followed a similar pattern. The Bud Moore pairing

Michigan International Speedway. A new 1969 SportsRoof appeared in Round 1 of the Trans-Am Championship for independent racer William Lowell, who'd hauled all the way from California. His race lasted just three laps, when he was black flagged for going off course.
(Courtesy Ron Lathrop)

of Jones and Follmer qualified at the front, along with Mark Donohue's Penske Camaro. A Jones/Donohue/Follmer battle for the lead would develop in the early laps, then the Mustangs' tire life would drop-away. The Firestones needed replacing more often than the Goodyears. Or, in the case of Circuit Mont-Tremblant, three of the four factory Mustangs were caught up in the lap-14 wreck. Of the 12 1969 Trans-Am Championship races, the Penske Camaros of Donohue and Ronnie Bucknum won eight, including all of the last seven. Despite having double the fire-power of Penske, and having spent considerably more money (an estimated $3.8 million), Ford trailed home bridesmaids for the second year in a row.

Smokey Yunick's Kar-Kraft Mustang was supplied as a complete car, finished in his familiar black and gold paint scheme. It was built in Trans-Am spec, but Knudsen requested him to convert it for NASCAR Grand Touring. It had its one and only race in Yunick's care at the opening event of Bill France's epic new Talladega Superspeedway in September, 1969. Competing in the Bama 400 Grand Touring race, which preceded the Grand National, driver

Bunky Blackburn qualified fastest. He led for much of the first third of the race, before engine failure put him out.

Allan Moffat took his Kar-Kraft Mustang to Australia and posted a win in a non-championship race on May 4, 1969, making this the first win anywhere for a 1969 Kar-Kraft Mustang. Because the now five-race championship began in March, he missed the first two races, but he also failed to finish any of the remaining three. His car was supplied with a 1968 tunnel-port motor, which was soon replaced with a Boss 302. Ian Geoghegan won the Australian Touring Car Championship for the fourth year in succession, still aboard his 1967 Mustang.

Michigan International Speedway. Maurice 'Mo' Carter powers his Camaro along the Michigan banking in practice, while George Follmer looks contemplative as he stands alongside his sleek new 1969 racer. Like Revson, Follmer drove a factory AMC Javelin in the 1968 Trans-Am before switching to the Ford squad to drive for Bud Moore. Unlike previous years where a variety of drivers were plugged into the Fords at different events, Follmer and Jones were a constant throughout 1969. They made a formidable partnership. *(Courtesy Ron Lathrop)*

Michigan International Speedway. Moments after the start, the field streams around the speedway banking. The 3.31-mile Michigan layout combined sections of the speedway with tricky road course sections, using both the infield out outfield. It wasn't popular with the drivers, particularly the abrupt connections between the banked oval and road course. To make matters worse, it rained, and snowed! *(Courtesy Ron Lathrop)*

Michigan International Speedway. Follmer, Mark Donohue, and Revson lap the 1968 Pontiac Firebird of Dick Brown through the infield. The helicopter in the background was required after Horst Kwech's Mustang left the track where the road course crossed the oval. He slid across the sodden grass, through a catch fence, and into a spectator area where he collided heavily with several parked cars. Tragically, an American Motors dealer, sitting in one of the cars, was killed as a result of the impact. *(Courtesy Ron Lathrop)*

103

Michigan International Speedway. Early in the race, following a violent spin in the wet after having started on dry tires, pole-sitter Jones pitted to fit wets. In trying to make up time, he went barrelling into Bert Everett's Porsche, punching in the front of the Mustang, and doing far worse damage to the Porsche. *(Courtesy Ron Lathrop)*

Michigan International Speedway. Revson, driving the number 1 Shelby Mustang, had his race cut short when a tire blew. *(Courtesy Ron Lathrop)*

Michigan International Speedway. As the track dried, Jones pitted once more to fit dry tires ... (see overleaf)

... his once-pristine Mustang is now sporting more damage, having run into another car during his recovery.

After the crew have bolted on the new tires, Bud Moore slams the roof to set Parnelli loose once more.

(Courtesy Ron Lathrop)

Michigan International Speedway. Following the race, Jones' Mustang looks ready for the wrecking yard. Lap counters had declared Mark Donohue the winner, having got completely confused from the numerous pit stops throughout the race as cars switched between wet and dry tires, in addition to refuelling. Four hours after the award ceremony, the result was overturned, as the Bud Moore team offered up evidence of its lap scoring. As such, Parnelli Jones was finally recognized as the winner, with this, the race-winning car. *(Courtesy Ron Lathrop)*

Australia. Bob Jane procured one of the 1968 Shelby Racing Co Trans-Am Mustangs to contest the 1969 Australian Touring Car Championship. This was the same car used to test the Gurney-Weslake setup at Riverside in late 1968. It was still fitted with the tunnel-port engine. The 1969 ATCC switched from a single-race event to a five-round series. Jane won the opening round, but failed to finish any of the remaining four events. Note the car is fitted with bumpers. This was a requirement of the Australian regulations. Giving chase at Calder Park, which Bob Jane owned, is Jane's older 1967 Mustang, being driven by John Harvey, and Terry Allan's 396in³ big block Camaro. *(Courtesy Oldracephotos/Simpson)*

Australia. Allan Moffat was gifted this 1969 Kar-Kraft Mustang (9F02M148624) by Jacque Passino. Canadian-born Moffat had proven himself a valuable team member for Ford Motor Company, dating back to 1964 with a Lotus Cortina. He was the second and last driver to win a Trans-Am race outright with a U2 car, when he took victory in the 1966 Bryar Trans-Am. Moffat had lived in Australia as a teenager, and felt there was good potential to build a career there, with Ford's help. In early 1969, he approached Passino about the idea of taking a Mustang to Australia, which was ultimately approved. Expecting to receive a 1968 notchback, he was instead gifted this car, much to his delight. It was fitted with a tunnel-port engine initially. It took its first victory at Sandown Park on May 4, 1969; the first race win for any of the 1969 Kar-Kraft Mustangs. Unlike the Kar-Kraft Mustangs contesting the Trans-Am, this car retained its 2in nose droop throughout its racing life. *(Courtesy Oldracephotos/Simpson)*

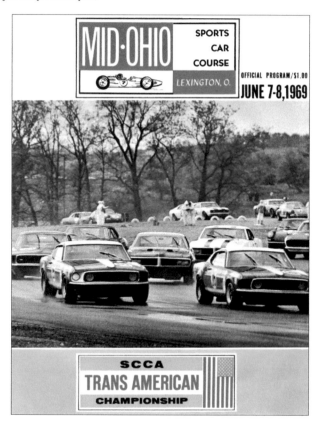

Mid-Ohio. Round 3 of the 1969 Trans-Am Championship was held at Mid-Ohio. Here the two Bud Moore Mustangs rest in the pits. From this angle can be seen the laser-straight bodywork and beautifully crafted fender flares, made by hammer and dolly. The way Jones and Follmer beat on these cars, the body team would have been kept busy. *(Courtesy Ron Lathrop)*

Several factors contributed to the outcome of the 1969 Trans-Am. One of them was tires. In 1969, Goodyear produced a better tire than Firestone. Both offered similar performance over a single lap, but the Goodyear was significantly more durable. Penske Racing and Shelby Racing Co used Goodyears, while Bud Moore used Firestones. A single set of Goodyears could often last an entire race, whereas the Firestones performance would drop off after a handful of laps, requiring replacements at each pit stop. *(Courtesy Ron Lathrop)*

Mid-Ohio. Pace lap for the Mid-Ohio Trans-Am race, and heated rivals Parnelli Jones and Mark Donohue share the front row, followed by Follmer, Revson, Kwech, Ronnie Bucknum (Penske Camaro), and the rest.
(Courtesy Ron Lathrop)

Mid-Ohio. Opening lap, and Jones and Donohue immediately pull out a small margin over the chasing pack, headed by Revson, John Martin (Javelin), Jerry Titus (Firebird), Follmer, Kwech, and Bucknum.
(Courtesy Ron Lathrop)

Mid-Ohio. Over the crest between turns nine and ten, many of the cars would get airborne, much more so the factory cars than the independents. Often, the Bud Moore drivers in particular kept the throttle wide open while the cars were in the air. *(Courtesy Ron Lathrop)*

Opposite, top left: Mid-Ohio. Jim Harrell is pictured heading under one of the Mid-Ohio pedestrian bridges. His race ended ten laps short of full distance with suspension failure. This was one of the first 1969 SportsRoof A/Sedan/Trans-Am Mustangs built, outside those of the factory teams. *(Courtesy Ron Lathrop)*

Opposite, top right: Mid-Ohio. Revson and Bucknum battle for the minor places early in the race as they lap Wilbur Pickett's Porsche. Ultimately, it was Bucknum who won, coming from nowhere thanks to slick Penske pit stops, good tire life, and Jones and Donohue wearing each other out at the front. This was the first race win in 1969 for Penske Racing. *(Courtesy Ron Lathrop)*

Mid-Ohio. Jones and Donohue were this close for lap after lap. The rivalry between the pair intensified throughout the year, and typified the 1969 season. Their heated duels were a highlight, and a benefit of the increased factory involvement in Trans-Am. When the checkered flag fell after 100 laps, neither was in front. Their battle ultimately disadvantaged both.
(Courtesy Ron Lathrop)

Mid-Ohio. Follmer's Mustang shows the tell-tale signs of having tangled with another car, which the Bud Moore drivers regularly did. In this case, it was the lapped Bob Bailey/Jim Locke U2 Porsche. Most of the slower drivers knew it was beneficial to make plenty of space when the factory cars came through. *(Courtesy Ron Lathrop)*

Mid-Ohio. Of the factory Mustang drivers, Revson usually brought his back straightest, but even on the twisty undulating Mid-Ohio course, he managed to rough-up a few other cars. *(Courtesy James R Gauerke/Ron Lathrop)*

Mid-Ohio. It was rare that Jones' Mustang didn't sport some form of body damage in 1969, but at Mid-Ohio, he kept it clean. Note the mixed wheels front to rear. The prototype 1969 Kar-Kraft Mustang was initially fitted with American Racing Torq-Thrust wheels, which most teams used in 1968. But by the opening 1969 race, the Mustangs were sporting the latest American Racing 200-S 'daisy' wheels. Following problems with these, most switched to the eight-spoke Minilite from England. At Mid-Ohio, both of the Bud Moore cars ran a combination of Minilites in front and American Racing 200-S wheels in the rear. *(Courtesy James R Gauerke)*

Mid-Ohio. Late in the race, Jones and Follmer put a lap on Dick Lang's Camaro. This would be one of several races that got away from the Bud Moore team in 1969 which they probably should have won. Ultimately, Jones and Follmer finished second and third. *(Courtesy Ron Lathrop)*

Charlie Kemp, pictured at Selma, Alabama, in SFM5R538, first raced by Roger West. Kemp purchased the GT350 in late 1967, and, with help from Pete Hood, developed and raced it extensively through 1971. Notable was the very low nose, with heavy rake. The pair also installed a full roll cage. Kemp contested 54 races with the Shelby, of which he won 32, including a winning streak of 17 in a row. At Daytona, this car reached 184mph, the highest-known speed for a 289 Shelby GT350 in period. SFM5R538 was documented as the 'winningest' Shelby GT350 race car ever.

(Courtesy Charlie Kemp Collection)

Bridgehampton. Pace lap for the 1969 Bridgehampton Trans-Am, and the Bud Moore and Shelby Mustangs have locked out the two front rows. Notable for their absence are the Penske Racing Camaros. After qualifying fastest, Donohue's Penske Camaro broke its engine during race-day warm-up, so he commandeered team-mate Bucknum's car, and started off the back in position 31. By lap 20, he was on the rear bumper of Follmer's second-placed Mustang, who was just behind Jones. The trio battled until Donohue slowed when his Chevy dropped to seven cylinders, while Jones retired a few laps shy of the end when his wiring harness caught fire. Follmer took the win, from Donohue. *(Courtesy Revs Institute, Albert R Bochroch)*

Circuit Mont-Tremblant. Circuit Mont-Tremblant was costly for Ford. Having already destroyed a car in the Michigan race, and heavily damaged another at Donnybrook, three more were caught up in the same wreck at Circuit Mont-Tremblant, when Follmer's engine blew and he spun on his own oil. Lax flag marshalling ensured he was soon joined in a pile of wrecked cars that included the Mustangs of Revson and Kwech, and Vic Campbell's Firebird. Of the front-runners, only Donohue and Jones escaped the carnage. Jones had already retired on lap nine, while Donohue was ahead of the chaos when it happened, and went on to take another victory. *(Courtesy Yves St-Jean)*

Kent. Dan Gurney was brought in to drive the number 2 Shelby Racing Co Mustang at Kent. His was a character-building race, suffering several punctures from the sharp rocks bordering the track, plus a broken windshield from rocks flicked up by other drivers, and, finally, a broken rear axle. He finished tenth, 11 laps down on eventual winner Bucknum. *(Courtesy Phil Rhodes)*

Kent. Carroll Shelby looks on, perhaps pondering life beyond racing. Following Kent, just two Trans-Am races remained. By 1969, Shelby's only racing program was the Trans-Am, and that was nearing an end. *(Courtesy Phil Rhodes)*

Kent. Canadian John Hall's independent 1968 Mustang notchback sits in the Kent pitlane. He retired from the race with suspension issues. *(Courtesy Phil Rhodes)*

Kent. Parnelli's office. The grey flooring is actually a tailored heat barrier mat made from asbestos welding blanket and fitted to the Bud Moore cars running from the front of the seat supports to the footwell. The steering wheel is a Grant. *(Courtesy Dave Friedman)*

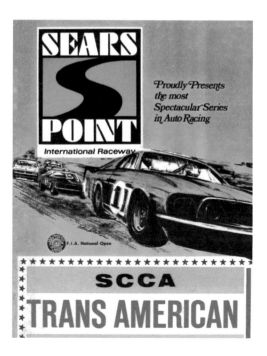

Talladega. NASCAR president Bill France opened his colossal new Talladega Superspeedway in September 1969. The main drawcard for the debut event was the Grand National stock car race, to be held Sunday September 14, but as a curtain-raiser, there was a NASCAR Grand Touring race, the Bama 400, held the day prior. 40 cars started the 151 lap race, and on pole was Bunky Blackburn in Smokey Yunick's 1969 Kar-Kraft Mustang (VIN 9F02M148626). Blackburn led a total 53 laps before engine failure on lap 56. This was the only race the Mustang contested under Yunick's care. *(Courtesy Revs Institute, Bruce R Craig)*

1970

The SCCA Trans-Am Championship peaked in 1970. Finally, all four major American auto makers were onboard, and in some cases, were financing multiple ventures. Millions of dollars in manufacturer money was being funnelled into what was now one of the most prominent racing championships in the world.

After its modest involvement in the inaugural Trans-Am season in 1966, Chrysler returned in 1970 with a serious two-pronged attack, and boasting one of the biggest names in the sport. Dan Gurney's All-American Racers (AAR) fielded a pair of Plymouth Cudas, driven by Gurney himself, and his young protégé Swede Savage. Meanwhile, Chrysler decided to hedge its bets, by funding a second team. Ray Caldwell's Autodynamics and Sam Posey partnered up to run a factory Dodge Challenger for Posey.

Chrysler went all-out in its Trans-Am effort, homologating a stack of components for the race cars through a pair of outlandish road cars; the AAR Cuda and Challenger T/A.

Roger Penske made the switch from Chevrolet to American Motors in a lucrative multi-year deal to run the factory Javelins, driven by Mark Donohue and Peter Revson. The Chevrolet Trans-Am program was taken over by sports car racing legend Jim Hall, and his celebrated Chaparral team. Hall enlisted himself to drive one of the Camaros, with Ed Leslie in the other. Jerry Titus was at the helm of the lone factory T/G Racing Pontiac Firebird. Like the Chaparral Camaros, these were the new-generation models.

Ford was back, of course, with Bud Moore Engineering entering a pair of 1970-model Mustangs, with his two brawlers Parnelli Jones and George Follmer retained once more to do the driving.

It was all very exciting.

Beneath the glossy exterior, however, Ford Motor Company was already beating a retreat. It was well advanced with major cut-backs to its racing involvement, and, more so, the money it was spending. The exorbitant Ford GT40/MkII/MkIV Le Mans project ended in 1967, and by the end of 1969, the NASCAR stock car and NHRA drag racing programs were also consigned to history. The racing budget had been slashed by a reported 75% for 1970.

All that was left was Trans-Am, but even in Trans-Am there were casualties. Ford budgeted an estimated $1 million for the 1970 Trans-Am series, but that was still insufficient to properly fund two teams. Shelby Racing Company got the axe, with Bud Moore Engineering now flying solo.

1970 Trans-Am regulations were subjected to more tweaks, notable among them the banning of multiple carburettors. Now, teams all had to make do with a single four-barrel, and that was it. Minimum weight increased to 3200lb, perhaps in an effort to stop all the acid-dipping and other expensive weight-loss stunts. It didn't really make a difference. The factory teams still invested in getting their cars as light as possible, so they could ballast them back up again.

Bud Moore Engineering prepared three 1970 Mustangs for the new Trans-Am season, although they weren't actually 1970 models at all. Chassis' 9F02M212775, 9F02M212776, and 9F02M212777 were all 1969 bodies updated and presented as 1970 cars. Both 775 and 776 were newly built, while 777 saw duty in late 1969, before being refurbished and updated as a 1970 model.

Kar-Kraft developed a new three-link rear suspension layout, but this was short-lived, and the cars quickly reverted back to the 1968/1969 rear suspension design. It appears Jones jumped between 775 and 777 at various times, while Follmer, for the most part, drove 776.

Having used two giant Holley four-barrel carburettors in 1969, the switch to a single 780cfm for 1970 brought with it a surprising horsepower increase, and much better driveability than the on/off reactions of the 1969 setup.

The Bud Moore Mustangs sported a fresh new color-scheme; factory Grabber Orange, which was affectionately dubbed Schoolbus Yellow. Once again, Jones would wear the number 15, and Follmer number 16, as they had done in 1969.

In July, 1969, Kar-Kraft engineers Lee Dykstra and Mitch Marchi tested perfectly detailed 3⁄8-scale model 1969 Mustang Trans-Am cars in the University

Daytona. The annual Daytona 24 Hours race had always been a popular challenge for small independent teams, sharing track space with the professional Prototype cars. The first and last time the Trans-Am Championship included Daytona was 1968, but the event remained a huge drawcard for sedan teams. Among the 65-car entry in 1970 was the number 94 Shelby GT350 of Don Cummings and Warren Stumes, competing in GT+2.0 (GT Over 2000cc), and the number 83 Mustang of Vince Collins and Larry Wilson, competing in T+2.0 (Touring Over 2000cc). Cummings/Stumes failed to finish, while Collins/Wilson were classified 26th from 27 finishers. *(Courtesy Autosportsltd.com)*

of Maryland wind tunnel. They trialled various spoilers and spoiler positions, plus a car fitted with a 1970 front, to see how it performed. From their findings, they produced full-scale components of those fitted to the 3/8-scale model, and attached them to a race car, also equipped with a 1970 front. This they extensively tested at the Martin-Marietta Lockheed wind tunnel in Marietta, Georgia.

Among their findings from the wind tunnel testing, they were able to trial angle and length of the front spoiler, and angle of the new-for-1970 rear spoiler, and how these components functioned at various speeds and under various loads.

The SCCA loosened its grip on brake regulations for 1970. Teams were now free to use any brakes they wished, no longer requiring they be from the same manufacturer. The Bud Moore Mustangs were thus equipped with Kelsey-Hayes brakes. In addition, any front spoiler could now be fitted, regardless of whether or not it was available on the road car, providing it was within the SCCA parameters.

Eleven rounds made up the 1970 Trans-Am Championship, and the Bud Moore duo won six of them; Jones took five victories, and Follmer one. For the most-part, the Mustangs were the fastest cars over a full race distance. On several occasions they were headed off in qualifying. Swede Savage was particularly impressive at nailing down a dynamite single lap, but in the races, Jones and Follmer often asserted themselves at the front to engage in a fiery inter-team battle for the win. Bud Moore Engineering wrapped up the 1970 Trans-Am Manufacturers' Championship with one race remaining.

Nobody could have foreseen it at the time, but 1970 was as good as it would ever get for the Trans-Am. Its ascent was relatively swift; its descent even more so. But while it teetered at the top, the Trans-Am was a spectacle of epic proportions.

Across the pond, in Great Britain, the British Saloon Car Championship switched from FIA Group 5 regulations to Group 2. Moving away from the liberal

Group 5 regulations meant the ultra-lightweight Ford Falcon Sprints which had dominated the series since 1966, were now outlawed. But American V8 heavy metal still prevailed.

The most prominent cars to feature in the 1970 BSCC were the Boss 302 Mustangs of Frank Gardner and Dennis Leech, and the Chevrolet Camaro of Brian Muir. Indeed, both the Gardner and Muir cars were former Trans-Am factory racers; Gardner's a 1969 Bud Moore Kar-Kraft Mustang (with updated 1970 nose), and Muir's a 1968 Penske Racing Camaro.

Gardner won eight of the 12 races, and Muir won three. Curiously, the 1970 British Saloon Car Championship was awarded to Bill McGovern, driving a tiny 998cc Hillman Imp. The BSCC points system rewarded Class results, not outright results, and over the course of the season, the Imp driver accumulated 72 Class points to the 68 Class points of Gardner.

The Group 2 regulations used in the BSCC allowed greater freedoms to those of the Trans-Am series. Cars could be fitted with larger engines and wider wheels and tires. That said, both the Gardner Mustang and Muir Camaro retained their 5-litre Trans-Am engines in 1970. Most V8 cars competing in the 1970 BSCC were fitted with wheels up to 10in wide, which required the fenders be extravagantly flared to house them.

There was little change to the Australian Touring Car Championship regulations, other than a new rule allowing cars to be fitted with wheels up to 10in wide. Previously, the limit was 8in.

From the seven Championship races, Allan Moffat took pole position four times in his Kar-Kraft Mustang, but converted only one of them into a race win. His Championship campaign was struck down by mechanical failures. After winning the opening race, he finished third in Round 3, and failed to go the distance in the other five races. The 1970 ATCC was won by Norm Beechey, driving a Holden Monaro GTS350, an Australian-made muscle car factory-fitted with a 350in³ small block Chevy.

Brands Hatch, England. After four years of FIA Group 5 regulations, the 1970 British Saloon Car Championship reverted back to Group 2 for 1970. This attracted a fleet of new machinery to the series, including the Mustangs of Frank Gardner (left) and Dennis Leech, and the Camaro of Brian Muir. Both the Gardner and Muir machines were former Trans-Am factory cars. The BSCC features standing starts, which can be quite dramatic. *(Courtesy McKlein Image Database)*

Oulton Park, England. Frank Gardner campaigned this Mustang in the 1970 British Saloon Car Championship. It was a 1969 Bud Moore factory Trans-Am car (9F02M148625), updated with 1970 front bodywork. Note the non-factory side marker light. Gardner won eight of the 12 races in 1970. He'd driven for Alan Mann Racing up until the end of 1969, when Mann closed his shop. For 1970, Gardner established Motor Racing Research with race car designer Len Bailey, and other ex-Mann employees. The Mustang was believed to have been paid for by Ford Britain. *(Courtesy Robert Clayson)*

Australia. For 1970, the Australian Improved Production regulations were adjusted to allow wheel widths to be increased from 8in to 10in. Allan Moffat is pictured here with his Kar-Kraft Mustang, being chased by Bryan Thomson in his big block 427in³ Camaro. Moffat had a tough year in the ATCC. After winning the opening race, a single third place was all he amassed.

(Courtesy John Stanley)

George Follmer (left) joins Parnelli Jones to form a potent Team Mustang driver combination in the 1970 SCCA Trans-Am Championship for sedans.

FROM: News Department, Ford Motor Company, The American Road, Dearborn, Michigan 48121 — Telephone: (313) 322-9600

IMMEDIATE RELEASE

Bryar. The 1970 Trans-Am was the best supported and most colourful yet. Finally, Chrysler entered with not one but two fully-fledged factory teams. At Bryar, Round 3 of the series, Swede Savage placed his AAR Plymouth Cuda on the outside front row, alongside Parnelli Jones' Bud Moore Mustang. Just behind are Mark Donohue in the Penske Racing factory Javelin, and Sam Posey in the factory Dodge Challenger. The two Chaparral Camaros lock out the third row. An exciting new look, indeed, but when the checkered flag fell, the result was a familiar one, with the Bud Moore and Penske cars filling the first three positions.

(Courtesy Autosportsltd.com)

By 1970, Shelby GT350s were still a popular choice in SCCA B/Production. After success in both A/Production and B/Production with his Shelby Cobra (CSX 2473) from 1966 through 1968, Don Roberts raced this 1966 Shelby GT350 (SFM6S2363) in 1970, further adding to his achievements. Roberts won the 1970 SCCA Southern Pacific Division B/Production Championship with this car. *(Courtesy Wayne Hill)*

Parnelli Jones' pristine Mustang arrives on the back of the Bud Moore hauler, ready to do battle. Rarely did Parnelli's race cars leave the track looking this straight. *(Courtesy Raynald Bélanger)*

Opposite, left: Mid-Ohio. Despite boasting million-dollar budgets, the factory teams still had to make do with the same modest pit paddocks as everyone else. A simple rope keeps onlookers at bay from the Bud Moore cars. The team took a third Mustang to several races in 1970. The man in the grey jacket is Fran Hernandez, head of Ford's racing programs. Hernandez attended most Trans-Am races in 1970. *(Courtesy Raynald Bélanger)*

Opposite, right: Mid-Ohio. In the Mid-Ohio paddock. The little guy in the car is likely Parnelli's son, PJ, who was born in April 1969. *(Courtesy Raynald Bélanger)*

Mid-Ohio. George Follmer is suited and booted, and ready for battle. And a battle he would have. After leading briefly, he was black-flagged for failing to slow for yellow flags. Making up ground, he stormed back through the field, eventually catching his team-mate with 12 laps remaining, igniting a furious scrap for the race win.

(Courtesy Raynald Bélanger)

Mid-Ohio. Follmer comes under attack from Swede Savage in the lone AAR Cuda. Mid-season Chrysler budget cuts meant Dan Gurney reduced to a single-car effort for much of 1970. Savage was leading at Mid-Ohio, before an oil leak put him out on lap 61.

(Courtesy Autosportsltd.com)

Mid-Ohio. Pit stop for Jones. Having led early, he slammed into a lapped Mustang, crushing the nose of his Bud Moore car, but was in front again when Savage retired. He was caught late in the race by his team-mate, and even though there was no Drivers' Championship, there was pride to play for. Follmer tried to get by; Jones ensured he didn't. The pair were separated by 0.3 seconds at the end of the 180-mile race. *(Courtesy Autosportsltd.com)*

MARLBORO TRANS-AM

BRIDGEHAMPTON RACE CIRCUIT
JUNE 20-21, 1970
OFFICIAL PROGRAM / $1.00

Bridgehampton. Racing among the sand dunes. Jones leads Mark Donohue's Penske Javelin. It began to rain early in the race, and the AMC driver surged ahead to take his first victory of the year, and the very first for American Motors since joining the Trans-Am in 1968. Jones finished third after spinning in the wet. *(Courtesy Autosportsltd.com)*

Circuit Mont-Tremblant. Bud Moore planned to run three cars at Circuit Mont-Tremblant, with A J Foyt in the spare. Foyt posted the 11th fastest qualifying time, but complained the car was handling poorly. Jones then ran some hot laps in Foyt's car, and promptly reversed it into the earth banking, causing enough damage for Foyt to be a non-starter. This is the same car raced by Shelby Racing Co in 1969, and driven for much of the year by Peter Revson. *(Courtesy Autosportsltd.com)*

Circuit Mont-Tremblant. During practice, the Bud Moore pairing of Jones and Follmer test the limits of their cars. Jones lifts his inside front wheel as he crests the Turn 1 rise.

(Courtesy Autosportsltd.com)

Circuit Mont-Tremblant. The 37-car grid is waved off to commence its pace lap. Old foes Jones and Donohue share the front row, followed by Follmer and Ed Leslie (Chaparral Camaro), Posey and Savage, Elford and Revson.

(Courtesy Autosportsltd.com)

Circuit Mont-Tremblant. Powering across the stripe to complete lap one, and Jones has already gapped the chasing pack, headed by Donohue. *(Courtesy Autosportsltd.com)*

Circuit Mont-Tremblant. Cars entered the pits at full speed, and although Bud Moore holds out a warning sign to Jones (Pit Slick), his driver still half-spun in the wet. While the track was dry, drainage problems meant the pit lane was wet, catching out several drivers. *(Courtesy Autosportsltd.com)*

Circuit Mont-Tremblant. Having wrecked his 1968 notchback, Dean Gregson built a new 1969 SportsRoof, into which he transferred many of the components from his wrecked car. The 1969 Mustang was a Mach 1 modified to look like a Boss 302. Gregson didn't travel far from his home-base in Rhode Island, so only contested the 1969 Circuit Mont-Tremblant Trans-Am race. For 1970, he updated the Mustang with a '70 nose, and ran both Lime Rock and Bridgehampton Trans-Ams, before coming here to Circuit Mont-Tremblant. He qualified 12th and finished 13th. *(Courtesy Autosportsltd.com)*

Circuit Mont-Tremblant. Pit stops were high drama in the Trans-Am, and increasingly, with the cars all being so close in performance, chunks of time could be made in the pits. Without the tire problems of 1969, the Firestone-shod Bud Moore cars didn't require replacements every time they stopped for gas. Here, Bud Moore, with fire extinguisher in hand, controls Jones while his car is fuelled. One team member releases the cap and another dumps the fuel. Meanwhile, another crew member hands Jones a drink. In the yellow shirt, Fran Hernandez times the stop. Once the car is full, Moore signals his driver to go, by bashing the hood. Trans-Am regulations stated only hand-held dump cans could be used for fueling in 1970, along with screw-in caps, to avoid the monstrous (and dangerous) high-volume towers that were being constructed in 1969. (Courtesy Autosportsltd.com)

Circuit Mont-Tremblant. Mark Donohue laps the Mustang of Steve Ross. This Mustang was owned and built by Jim Bell and Sonny Barron, who worked at New York Ford dealer Judge Motors. Barron, a short-track speedway racer, was to drive the Mustang, but as he was unable to get his license in time, Ross was drafted in to drive the car at Circuit Mont-Tremblant. In the unfamiliar car, Ross qualified 34th, and finished 20th. *(Courtesy Autosportsltd.com)*

Circuit Mont-Tremblant. Thanks to a clever Penske Racing pit strategy, Donohue made his first stop on lap 14, a full ten laps earlier than his rivals. The Penske stops were the fastest on the pit lane, and the Javelin was the fastest car on the track in the second half of the race. After lap 14, Donohue didn't see another front-running car all day, and Roger Penske kept his driver informed of his lead late in the race. 'Fumbler' refers to Follmer, who at the time was 17 seconds in arrears, and never caught up. Jones was third. The Bud Moore team had been outmaneuvered at Circuit Mont-Tremblant. *(Courtesy Autosportsltd.com)*

Watkins Glen. Inside Follmer's Bud Moore Mustang. The staggered layout of the gauges suggests this is chassis 777. Both 775 and 776 had the gauges all in a horizontal line. *(Courtesy Randy Hernandez)*

Watkins Glen. Fran Hernandez, pictured in the light blue shirt, was manager of Ford's racing programs in 1970. He knew his way around a race car, having been involved in the sport all his life. Following WW2 he'd partnered with Fred Offenhauser to form Offenhauser Equipment Corporation. He then worked for Vic Edelbrock, building, among other things, Ford V8-60 motors running on nitromethane for Midget racing. So successful were these engines, they even beat Offenhauser's pure-bred Offy motors. He was himself a keen drag racer, and one of the pioneers of the sport. It was while with Edelbrock he began working with Bill Stroppe, which was when he first began doing work for Ford Motor Company, building the Lincolns to run La Carrera Panamericana. In the early 1960s, he headed the Lincoln-Mercury racing program, and was responsible for bringing Bud Moore across to Ford Motor Company, initially running NASCAR stock cars, NHRA drag cars, and then the SCCA Trans-Am. *(Courtesy Randy Hernandez)*

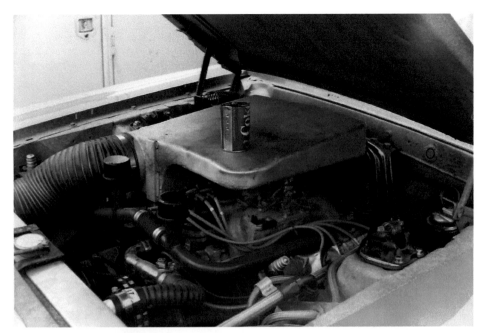

Watkins Glen. The engine room in Follmer's Bud Moore Mustang. 1970 Trans-Am rules allowed only a single four-barrel carburettor, which, with some work, actually produced more power for the Fords than the twin four-barrel setup in 1969. The aluminum air box feeds cold air direct from the nose of the car to the carburettor. The Fords had the most power of all the Trans-Am cars in 1970, at around 480 horsepower. It was common practice to paint the engine bay, interior, and underside of a Trans-Am car grey, to help show up any oil leaks. Whether or not it was intentional, it also made detecting cracks from too much acid-dipping easier too. *(Courtesy Randy Hernandez)*

Watkins Glen. Warren Tope's Mustang rests in the Watkins Glen paddock. His father, Donald Tope, headed Ford's transmission and chassis division, and as such, had access to cars and racing equipment. This car was first built in 1969, and with 1970 nose installed, ran selected 1970 Trans-Am races. It spent time at Kar-Kraft, and while not receiving the same treatment as the factory cars, was still well-built and afforded top-level equipment. *(Courtesy Randy Hernandez)*

Watkins Glen. Just prior to race start. Jones was on pole. He talks race tactics with Bud Moore. The Chaparral Camaro alongside is third fastest qualifier Vic Elford. (*Courtesy Randy Hernandez*)

Watkins Glen. Taking the race start, Jones jumps ahead of Donohue, Elford, Posey and Savage. This time it was Elford who won, profiting from rain that arrived at one-third distance, which his Camaro excelled in. Donohue was second, while Follmer stumbled across the line, out of fuel, in third. (*Courtesy Randy Hernandez*)

Watkins Glen. Comparison of two Ford-connected independent Mustangs of Dean Gregson and Warren Tope, cresting the Watkins Glen hill. (*Courtesy Autosportsltd.com*)

Dean Gregson's Mustang rounds the final turn at Watkins Glen to begin another lap. He qualified 26th, but failed to finish. Gregson was one of the few to use the six-spoke American Racing TA 70 magnesium wheels. Most teams opted for Minilites in 1970.

(Courtesy Autosportsltd.com)

Watkins Glen. Once again, Jones and Donohue battled hard for a race win, just as they had in previous races, and in previous years. They were fierce competitors, and Jones believed Donohue evolved into a better driver because of their rivalry. Sadly, their Trans-Am duels were nearing an end. Only two more races followed Watkins Glen, and Ford finally won back the Manufacturers' Championship, then promptly withdrew from the series. The heated Jones/Donohue contests were a highlight of the Trans-Am series at its peak.

(Courtesy Autosportsltd.com)

Hockenheim, Germany. In September 1970, one of several support races to the Formula A/5000 main event at Hockenheim, was for 'Stock Cars.' The race was organized by NASCAR Deutschland, and NASCAR president Bill France was listed as the Official Starter. There were no actual NASCAR stock cars in attendance, rather, only big-engined road course sedans that raced in Europe and Great Britain. The fastest three cars were the Mustangs of Dennis Leech and Frank Gardner, and Brian Muir's Camaro, which had all travelled from England. The Camaro in fourth is that of David Prophet, who also travelled from England.

(Courtesy Jim Culp)

Hockenheim, Germany. Dennis Leech took an initial lead in the Hockenheim Stock Car race, but blasted through one of the temporary foam chicanes on the long straights, designed to keep speeds down. He crossed the finish line first but was given a 30-second penalty for his misdemeanor. Chunks of the chicane can be seen in his grille. *(Courtesy Jim Culp)*

Hockenheim, Germany. With Leech disqualified, Frank Gardner, who crossed the line second, was declared the winner in his ex-Bud Moore Engineering Mustang. Gardner retained the Trans-Am 302 motor in the Mustang for 1970, but fitted the car with noticeably wider wheels and tires, which the regulations allowed in the British championship. *(Courtesy Jim Culp)*

143

Hockenheim, Germany. The only actual NASCAR driver to contest the one-off NASCAR Deutschland Stock Car race at Hockenheim was Tiny Lund. He drove a six-cylinder German Open Commodore, seen here chasing Martin Birrane's Mustang, and the Team Schnitzer BMW 2800CS of Ernst Furtmayr. Birrane was another to travel from England. His 1968 Mustang notchback was fitted with a 427in³ big block motor. (*Courtesy Jim Culp*)

New Zealand. In late 1970, New Zealand racer Paul Fahey began racing this Mustang SportsRoof. The car was actually a rare (500 made) 1970 Boss 429 road car which he'd purchased at a theft-recovery auction while on business in Los Angeles. Thieves had taken the engine and driveline. Fahey had an association with Carroll Shelby and several Shelby employees, including New Zealander Ron Butler. Butler gained Fahey access to the Shelby American workshops, which had ceased operation by 1970. With a stockpile of parts left over from the various racing programs, Fahey purchased everything available and shipped it back to New Zealand where he had the Mustang built into a race car, using parts from the Shelby stash. (*Courtesy Allan Cameron*)

1971

Seven months separated the final 1970 Trans-Am race at Riverside and the first 1971 race at Lime Rock Park, but it might as well have been seven years, such was the level of change that had taken place.

In 1970, the Trans-Am reached full blossom, with factory-supported teams representing all four of Detroit's major automotive manufacturers, and in some cases including multiple brands. Ford Mustang, Chevrolet Camaro, AMC Javelin, Plymouth Cuda, Dodge Challenger, and Pontiac Firebird all raced in an official capacity, ensuring an intense battle throughout the 1970 season, with Ford ultimately emerging as champion. In 1971, they'd all gone; except for American Motors, which still had two years left to run on its contract with Roger Penske.

The mass exodus was the result of a combination of several factors. Aside from the spiralling costs, the main contributor was simply a decline in pony car sales. The new generation of car buyers in 1971 wanted something different to those of 1964. By 1971, the pony car was seven years old. It was no longer new and fresh, and buyers' tastes were changing. It didn't make sense for manufacturers to pour millions of dollars into a race series when the market was shifting away from the very product they were racing.

Without Ford's significant financial contribution, Bud Moore Engineering continued on alone in 1971, using sponsorship and the sale of race cars to fund its season. Peter Gregg was recruited to drive the number 16 car. Gregg arranged much-needed funding from Florida building company S S Jacobs. Parnelli Jones was enlisted to drive the number 15 car once more, but after the opening race, George Follmer took his place.

The 1971 Bud Moore Mustangs were all-new cars – and they were also quite special. They were built from bodies in white that had been produced in late 1970 and were stamped from thin-gauge sheet metal. Clearly, at the time of their production, Ford was still in the game, and various employees within both Ford and Kar-Kraft were already looking ahead to the 1971 program. Four bodies were known to have been produced, and none of them received a Ford VIN.

As well as Bud Moore Engineering, there was also a handful of independent teams running ex-factory Mustangs, but Bud Moore's team was the only one to take a race victory (two, in fact), with Mark Donohue cleaning house in the Penske Javelin. Penske Racing wrapped up the Manufacturers' Championship for American Motors with a race to spare. Follmer had been courageous in the under-funded Mustang, and the only one to truly challenge the Penske car. Riverside is a long haul from South Carolina, with nothing to play for, so Bud Moore opted to skip the final race.

Allan Moffat probably should have been crowned 1971 Australian Touring Car Champion in his 1969 Kar-Kraft Mustang. He engaged in a fearsome battle with Bob Jane, who was driving a newly-constructed Camaro. The Australian regulations had no maximum engine size limit, and, as such, Jane raced a genuine 1969 Camaro ZL-1, with aluminum big block 427in^3 motor. No expense was spared in building the Camaro to the local regulations. Remarkably, Ian Geoghegan with his elderly 1967 Mustang was also in with a mathematical shot at winning the title, heading into the seventh and final race. After six events, Jane had 34 points, Geoghegan 32, and Moffat 31. The points system was the same as the Trans-Am: 9-6-4-3-2-1.

After six races, Moffat had won three, Jane two, and Geoghegan one. Whoever won the seventh race was assured of being crowned champion. Moffat was leading throughout the final, until his Toploader gearbox jammed in second gear, requiring him to stop his car so he could release it. Once he got going again, he was third, behind Geoghegan, and Jane, who was leading. Geoghegan fended off Moffat for several laps before he finally broke through and began a mighty comeback, reducing Jane's 18-second lead to nothing by the final lap. But it was all too late.

The outcome should have been different for Moffat. In Round 3, he was leading the race when assigned a black flag, as officials spotted something hanging down beneath the car, and wanted him to pit so they could check it. He continued to race on, ignoring the flag before finally pitting on the last lap. His car was inspected and he was sent back into the race. Such was his lead he still won by a significant margin, but he was later excluded from the results for not observing the flags, and Jane, running second at the end, was promoted to the win.

In 1970, it was the Penske Racing Javelin of Mark Donohue chasing the Bud Moore Mustangs in most races. In 1971, the roles were reversed. American Motors was the only manufacturer remaining in the 1971 Trans-Am, and Penske Racing the only truly well-funded team. *(Courtesy Autosportsltd.com)*

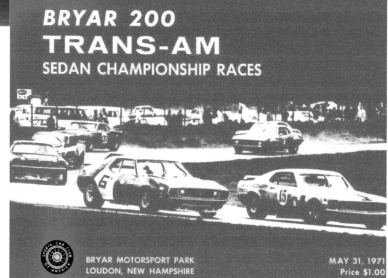

Although no longer enjoying Ford support, Bud Moore Engineering returned to the Trans-Am in 1971 with a pair of newly-built Grabber Orange Mustangs. Parnelli Jones drove for Moore in the opening race at Lime Rock, before George Follmer took over his car thereafter. Peter Gregg was recruited to drive the second car, and was responsible for bringing much-needed funding from Florida building company S S Jacobs. *(Courtesy Raynald Bélanger)*

For the past two years, Follmer was aboard a Bud Moore Mustang with a 16 on the door. In 1971, he raced the number 15 car. Although newly built, the 1971 Bud Moore Mustangs looked outwardly similar to the 1970 cars. The most obvious visual styling cues are the S S Jacobs lettering on the front fenders, and the white-painted Minilite wheels. *(Courtesy Autosportsltd.com)*

Follmer pits during the Bryar round of the 1971 Trans-Am. The
Bud Moore team is still as slick as ever, with Moore himself
(seen here with his back to camera holding the pit board) still
in charge of conducting the stops. *(Courtesy Autosportsltd.com)*

Follmer took a surprise victory at Bryar, after Donohue retired with
mechanical issues. Post-race he is flanked by Miss Bryar, and Joanne Carson,
Johnny Carson's wife. At the front of the Mustang is Cecil Moore, Bud's
brother. In the background is Ken Stoddart's stricken Camaro, which lost a
wheel on lap 55. The wheel bounced into the Bryar pond, forcing Stoddart to
wade in and fish it out. *(Courtesy Autosportsltd.com)*

Having enjoyed considerable success in SCCA A/Production sports car racing with a series of big block Corvettes, the pairing of Tony DeLorenzo and Jerry Thompson decided to get involved in the Trans-Am series in 1970. Their sponsor, Owens Corning Fibreglass, went with them, although some within the company couldn't see the value in racing steel bodied cars when Owens Corning was in the composites business. Of course, they built and raced Camaros. DeLorenzo's father was a long-time General Motors employee, eventually rising to head of public relations. The Camaro program was tough, suffering numerous delays and setbacks. When the cars finally hit the track, performance was disappointing. So for 1971, with new sponsor Troy Promotions, DeLorenzo and Thompson raced a pair of ex-factory Mustangs. DeLorenzo (number 3) raced 9F02M212777 (originally Peter Revson's 1969 Shelby car), and Thompson (number 4) raced 9F02M148628. Both had come from Bud Moore.

(Courtesy Autosportsltd.com/Raynald Bélanger)

Having raced a self-built Mustang in 1969 and 1970, Warren Tope purchased a Bud Moore Mustang (9F02M212776) for 1971, driven throughout much of 1970 by George Follmer. *(Courtesy Raynald Bélanger)*

Dean Gregson returned to the Trans-Am in 1971 with the Mustang he'd raced since 1969. Typically, Gregson raced only on the East Coast. *(Courtesy Autosportsltd.com)*

Warren Tope ran a second Mustang at selected events, for Gene Harrington. *(Courtesy Raynald Bélanger)*

Ed Hinchcliff built and raced this Mustang in 1970, starting with a body in white. He contested two Trans-Am races in 1970, and a further nine in 1971. His best result was seventh at Riverside.

(Courtesy Autosportsltd.com)

Ex-factory Trans-Am Mustangs, including the original Kar-Kraft prototype first raced by Shelby Racing Co in 1969 (9F02R112073), made their way into the hands of various independent teams in 1971. In 1971, it was run by Dark Horse Racing, driven by John Gimbel. Here Gimbel leads Dean Gregson's Mustang.

(Courtesy Autosportsltd.com)

152

Australia. The 1971 Australian Touring Car Championship was one of high-drama that went down to the wire. Allan Moffat in his 1969 Kar-Kraft Mustang, Ian Geoghegan in his 1967 Mustang, and Bob Jane in his newly-built 1969 Camaro all went into the final race with a chance to win. Jane's Camaro, pictured here chasing Moffat, was a genuine ZL-1, complete with aluminum big block 427in^3 motor. The championship was decided on the last corner of the last lap, in Jane's favor. *(Courtesy Oldracephotos/Simpson)*

Allan Moffat, pictured with his Mustang while racing in New Zealand.

(Courtesy Peter Hanna)

Great Britain. A new addition to the 1971 British Saloon Car Championship was the Mustang SportsRoof of Martin Birrane. This is the car built in 1970 by Don Eichstaedt and other Kar-Kraft employees for the Boss 302 Chassis Modification manual, which, much like Chevrolet had done with the Camaro in 1968, showed racers the various steps required, and the parts required, to build a Boss 302 road race car. This car was featured throughout the 30-page manual, which was highly detailed. Although it never contested a Trans-Am race, Eichstaedt ran the Grabber Orange Mustang in a handful of local SCCA A/Sedan races in late 1970, before Kar-Kraft was closed. It was then purchased by Birrane and taken to England. Fitted with vastly wider wheels, as allowed in the BSCC, Birrane takes a wild ride through the Silverstone infield during the GKN Trophy meeting. *(Courtesy Mike Hayward)*

New Zealand. Not a Bud Moore Mustang, but rather the PDL Mustang, from New Zealand. This is the same car Paul Fahey had started racing in late 1970, originally built from a Boss 429. In 1971, Fahey sold the car to PDL Electrical, but was retained as the driver. *(Courtesy Peter Hanna Collection)*

155

1972

By 1972, the SCCA Trans-Am series was on the ropes. When the factory teams withdrew, it reverted to what it had been in 1966: a championship for amateur drivers. The trouble was, after years of intense factory participation, nobody wanted to watch an amateur series any more. It couldn't go back to what it was in 1966 and expect to succeed.

Even at the best of times, the Trans-Am prize pool was modest. The real money was internal: car manufacturers paying contracted teams and drivers to represent their brands. So by 1972, when the factory teams had gone away, the Trans-Am didn't actually suffer so much for numbers. The trouble was, without Donohue, Jones and Follmer beating the stuffing out of each other with their state-of-the-art factory race cars, the showbiz had gone out of it.

There remained one factory team, of sorts, in 1972. American Motors still had a year remaining on its contract with Roger Penske, but Penske could see little value in hauling his car around the country to race a bunch of amateurs. So, with permission granted from head office, he handed the AMC Javelin program, along with its cars, spares, and setups, to Roy Woods Racing, which ran a pair of cars for Roy and George Follmer.

Meanwhile, Bud Moore Engineering had quit the series, and returned to the NASCAR Grand National, running a Ford for David Pearson. Mustang representation in Trans-Am was a collection of independents with their two- and three-year-old cars, some of which were former factory team cars.

Ironically, given the number of superstar drivers to have graced the Trans-Am since its inception, the SCCA waited until 1972 to finally include a Drivers' Championship.

Eleven rounds were originally scheduled for the 1972 Trans-Am Championship, but Follmer and American Motors had already wrapped up both the Drivers' and Manufacturers' Championships after six. Indeed, the series was thus shortened to seven rounds.

Warren Tope, driving an ex-Bud Moore factory Mustang, won two rounds, and ultimately finished third in the Drivers' Championship.

Things were a little more positive in both the British Saloon Car Championship and Australian Touring Car Championship. Dennis Leech decided the problem with his 1970 Mustang was a lack of horsepower, so he shoehorned a monster Boss 429 between the front shock towers. He didn't come close to winning a race, but it certainly provided a lot of interest.

Allan Moffat once again battled Bob Jane's Camaro for the ATCC, but Jane won again, prospering from too many mechanical failures for his adversary.

1972 was the last year for the existing Australian regulations, which had been in place since 1965. For 1973, a new format ensured only Australian-manufactured cars were eligible to race in the ATCC, and, as such, this exciting period of Australian motorsport history, and the mighty American cars that had played such a prominent role, came to an end.

Daytona. The big-body 1971-model Mustang, the last of the first generation, never raced in the original 1966-1972 era of the Trans-Am. But a few did compete in NASCAR Grand Touring, which, by 1972, NASCAR had re-branded Grand American. Al Straub and Norm Mosher shared this Grand American Mustang in the 1972 Daytona 6 Hours. Due to the energy crisis, the annual Daytona 24 Hours was shortened to just six hours. The Straub/Mosher Mustang retired after just two laps. (Courtesy Autosportsltd.com)

Sebring. Although they didn't contest any Trans-Am races in 1972 beyond the season-opener at Lime Rock, Tony DeLorenzo and Jerry Thompson teamed up for the Sebring 12 Hours. They qualified 24th outright, but engine failure ended their race after 116 laps. *(Courtesy Autosportsltd.com)*

Sebring. Manuel Quintana and John Belperche shared this 1968 Shelby GT350 in the Sebring 12 Hours, running in the GT+2.5 class. They crashed out of the race after qualifying 53rd. *(Courtesy Autosportsltd.com)*

Sebring. Neil Potter, Oran Ansley, and Bill Hood shared this ancient Mustang notchback in the 1972 Sebring 12 Hours. Races like this were still a popular place for low-buck enthusiasts to compete on a grand stage. They qualified 54th outright but engine failure ended their race. *(Courtesy Autosportsltd.com)*

Warren Tope continued racing his ex-Bud Moore Mustang in the 1972 Trans-Am. Now sporting a handsome new paint scheme, Tope scored a pair of victories at Road America and Sanair, in what would ultimately be the final two races for the Trans-Am in its original form. *(Courtesy Autosportsltd.com)*

SCHAEFER TRANS-AM
LIME ROCK PARK

MAY 6, 1971   ONE DOLLAR

Ed Hinchcliffe is pictured at Watkins Glen for the 1972 Trans-Am, where he was classified 16th.

(Courtesy Autosportsltd.com)

Having raced a Camaro in the 1971 Trans-Am, Marshall Robbins purchased two of the 1971 Bud Moore Mustangs, and raced a selection of Trans-Am and local SCCA A/Sedan events. Jerry Thompson also drove on occasion for Robbins in 1972. *(Courtesy Autosportsltd.com)*

John Gimbel continued in the 1972 Trans-Am with the Dark Horse Racing ex-factory Mustang. *(Courtesy Autosportsltd.com)*

Silverstone, England. Convinced a horsepower increase would help his performances against the new breed of Group 2 cars competing in the British Saloon Car Championship, Dennis Leech shoe-horned a Boss 429 engine into his Mustang (number 15). The monster engine didn't really help. His best result was third in Round 2 at Oulton Park. He battled reliability issues throughout much of the year. *(Courtesy Robert Clayson)*

The impressive powerplant in
Dennis Leech's Mustang: a Boss
429, complete with fuel-injection.
(Courtesy Shepherd Family)

New Zealand. Australian
international racer Frank
Gardner took his old Camaro
to New Zealand in late 1972,
where he met with several
top local and Australian
teams to race at Bay Park
and Pukekohe. The Camaro
had originally been raced in
the 1967 Trans-Am by Bobby
Brown, and continued to be
developed during its time in
England. Gardner enjoyed
success with the car in 1971,
before building a new, second
generation Camaro in 1972.
Here, he shares the front
row with Allan Moffat in his
Kar-Kraft Mustang. Unlike
the Kar-Kraft Mustangs that
contested the Trans-Am in
1969, Moffat's Mustang never
had its severe nose-droop
reduced. *(Courtesy Peter Hanna)*

1973-1986

By 1973, a new name had established itself in sports car/sedan road racing. It was called the International Motor Sports Association (IMSA) and it was created and presided by a familiar name, former SCCA Executive Director, John Bishop. NASCAR president Bill France owned a 25% share.

IMSA arrived as a true powerhouse, with sponsorship from R J Reynolds Tobacco Company brand Camel cigarettes to the tune of $300,000 for its GT series. France had already enticed R J Reynolds Winston cigarettes into the NASCAR Grand National in 1971.

Much as he had done at the SCCA, Bishop favored using FIA regulations, rather than cobbling together a home-brew that required constant adjustments to keep the masses happy. For IMSA GT, he went with FIA Groups 2 and 4, which attracted some of the top factory teams from Europe. Many of the old Trans-Am independents also participated, upgrading their cars to the latest Group 2 rules as they did so, but IMSA GT was dominated by the Europeans: Porsche and BMW.

So, in 1974, Bishop introduced a new category called All-American GT, in an effort to entice Detroit back to racing. It worked, to an extent, as Chevrolet supported a project to field full tube-frame Chevy Monzas that could contend for outright wins. Horst Kwech and Lee Dykstra, who'd formed DeKon Engineering, spearheaded the project, building turn-key cars for a variety of customers.

The IMSA Monzas bore almost no resemblance to their road-going namesakes, although they did utilize some body and roof sections from the actual road cars.

One potential DeKon Monza customer was Charlie Kemp, who decided he could build a better version of the Monza for AA-GT, but using a Mustang II body and Ford V8 engine. The Kemp Cobra II was controversial from the outset, and very fast. It collected multiple pole positions from 1976-1979, but for one reason or another, a race win proved elusive.

With the original Trans-Am having all but crumbled away by 1972, the SCCA followed a similar path to IMSA by adopting FIA regulations and focusing on a GT-concept, but it lacked the impressive IMSA prize purses, which in turn, meant it lacked the quality IMSA grids. As the 1970s rumbled on, the American automotive industry increasingly lost its way, and the supply of powerful factory performance cars had all but dried up. So it really wasn't possible to race what was being produced, even if there had been a willingness to do so. Remarkably, by 1978, the fastest accelerating American-made vehicle on the market was the Dodge Lil' Red Express custom pick-up truck. It accelerated faster than a Corvette from 0-100mph.

In the early 1980s, the SCCA started to fight back. A new-look model Trans-Am offered a link to the past, by introducing a stock-block V8 formula with maximum 5000cc engine capacity. Grids grew once more, and even the manufacturers got involved, to an extent. The new-generation Trans-Am cars utilized a tube-frame chassis design over which was draped heavily exaggerated composite body. The cars were fast and spectacular, but the fans never took to them like the cars of the original 1966-1972 era.

Meanwhile, in other parts of the world, a new FIA touring car formula called Group A was introduced in 1982, and quickly spread from Europe, to Great Britain, Australia and New Zealand. Group A was, in many respects, an evolution of Group 2. The cars were required to be production-based, mass-produced, and allowing a set number of modifications be carried out for the purposes of racing, such as the fitment of competition wheels, tires, suspension components, brakes, and exhaust systems. Bodywork had to remain completely stock. Furthermore, manufacturers could produce low-volume street examples to homologate specific components for the racing variants. This was, in essence, a modern day Group 2.

With Group A came a return to international racing for the Mustang. It appeared an unlikely fit, given the model was raced everywhere but the country in which it was created; the United States never adopted Group A.

Several third-generation Mustangs competed in Group A. The most

Charlie Kemp built this incredible tube-frame Mustang II (Kemp Cobra
II) to contest the IMSA All-American GT category, against the successful
DeKon Monzas. Kemp raced the Mustang for three years, from 1976, and
although he took several pole positions, race wins eluded him.
(Courtesy Autosportsltd.com)

successful of these were run by Peter Zakowski's German team, Zakspeed,
and by Australian Ford hero, Dick Johnson. Zakspeed had successfully
raced Ford products for several years, and enjoyed factory support from
Ford Motor Company. Indeed, Zakspeed sold two Group A Mustangs to
Johnson, who campaigned them in the 1985 and 1986 Australian Touring
Car Championships. In 1985, Johnson finished second in championship
points.

The addition of the Mustang name back in international racing was
met with great enthusiasm, but it never reached its potential as a Group
A racer, because its Ford 302in^3 V8, with its small cylinder ports, was
difficult to extract sufficient power from. After two years of development,
Johnson was coaxing around 350hp from his engines. The regulations
required the cars be fitted with the same cylinder heads as those on the
road cars, and limited the amount of modification that could be carried
out on the heads. Of course, Group A didn't operate in the United States,
and Detroit had no interest in producing a homologation special to make
the Mustang a more competitive car. Aerodynamically, it was highly
efficient, and displayed beautiful handling and braking capabilities, but it
lacked horsepower.

For 1987, Ford Europe took full advantage of the Group A regulations
to unleash a four-cylinder turbocharged Cosworth-powered variant
of the European Sierra, called the Sierra RS Cosworth. It was quickly
superseded by an even better weapon, the Sierra RS500. In Group A trim,
the best Sierra RS500s were pushing out well over 500hp, and more still
in qualifying mode with the boost turned up.

With the Sierra RS500 on the scene, Ford teams quickly upgraded
their equipment, and the Mustangs brief return to international racing
was soon consigned to history.

New Zealand. This car was built in 1976, by the PDL racing team in New Zealand to replace its old 1970 SportsRoof. It utilized some original Ford Mustang II body panels, much like the Kemp Cobra II, but was scratch-built around a tube-frame chassis. Kemp supplied the fiberglass bodykit. Power came from a fuel-injected 351in³ with aluminum engine block.

(Courtesy Ross Cammick and Rick Deihl)

In the early 1980s, the SCCA Trans-Am series attempted to capture some of the magic of the original 1966-1972 era by shifting away from FIA regulations, as used by rival sanctioning group IMSA, and returned to a stock-block V8 formula, limited to 5000cc. Where it differed from the original was that cars were now using a full tube-frame chassis with a composite silhouette body draped over the top. *(Courtesy Autosportsltd.com)*

IMSA cars by the early 1980s were wild. This is the Zakspeed Mustang, built and raced by Peter Zakowski's famed German racing team. The Mustang was essentially the exact same car raced by Zakspeed in the German Deutsche Rennsport Meisterschaft, but with a European Ford Capri body fitted. The DRM, like IMSA, used FIA Group 5 regulations.

(Courtesy Autosportsltd.com)

The Mustang made a surprise comeback in the 1980s in FIA Group A touring car racing. Group A was much like the original SCCA Trans-Am, in that cars were production-based, mass-produced, and were required to be homologated to be eligible to compete. Several teams raced Mustangs from 1983 until 1986, including Zakspeed in Germany. The most successful of these was Australian Ford racer Dick Johnson, who finished second in the 1985 Australian Touring Car Championship with this Zakspeed-built car. Because Group A was never adopted in the United States, Ford never homologated parts to help them be more successful. *(oldracephotos.com/Hammond)*

EPILOGUE

In 2014, the Ford Mustang turned 50. Today, it sells in greatly reduced numbers compared to the heady days of the 1960s, but as one of Ford's celebrated halo cars, and with history and tradition in its corner, survival is almost guaranteed.

However, it appears increasingly unlikely the model will ever be revered in racing circles as it was during the 1960s, when top-level sedan racing still bore a strong relationship to the cars people drove on the street. Mustang is represented in multiple modern day racing formulas with Ford's support and blessing, from NASCAR to the Australian Supercars Championship (formerly Australian Touring Car Championship), but modern day motorsport demands parity between brands, to ensure close racing. Close, exciting racing is what keeps the fans coming back – and the most effective way to achieve parity is to make all the brands the same, with no one model gaining an advantage.

This, then, requires a controlled chassis and key components shared throughout the manufacturers, with silhouette bodywork draped over the top, stretched and manipulated to fit. With warpaint and badges removed, the different brands are virtually indistinguishable, but the desired effect, close racing, is still achieved. The downside is that race fans can't relate to the cars, and nor can they fall in love with them. The cars bear little resemblance to those being sold in dealership showrooms, and as such, don't have the same direct influence on sales as those driven by Parnelli Jones and Mark Donohue, et al, in the 1960s. Modern racing ensures the drivers, and their personalities, are thrust into the limelight, and their association with a particular brand of car helps push sales for that brand. Indeed, racing still drives emotion, just as it has always done, but the way car manufacturers tap into those emotions is achieved in a different way.

It is fortuitous, then, that we have history to look back on and to celebrate. Because, in effect, modern racing is built on a platform whose foundations are entrenched in the past, and when it becomes difficult finding the link connecting modern racing and history, we can simply enjoy history for what it is. The Mustang's role in one of the most celebrated periods in sedan racing history, the 1960s, will always be a high point. Indeed, the Mustangs that raced in the 1960s and early 1970s were truly loved by race fans, just as much as the heroes who drove them, and, 50 years later, that love-affair shows little sign of letting up …

More from Veloce

Essential Buyer's Guides™ from Veloce's best-selling series

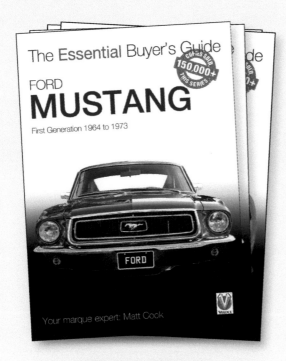

ISBN: 978-1-845844-47-9
Paperback • 19.5x13.9cm • 64 pages
• 106 colour pictures

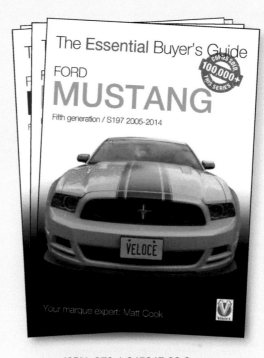

ISBN: 978-1-845847-98-2
Paperback • 19.5x13.9cm • 64 pages
• 108 colour pictures

Whichever car you're looking for, you can't go wrong with one of our Essential Buyer's Guides. Written by carefully chosen marque experts, these books will guide you through the process of finding, assessing and buying a range of aspirational and classic cars.
Benefit from the authors' years of ownership and experience, learn how to spot a bad car quickly, and how to assess a promising car like a professional. Get the right car at the right price!

To see the full range and for more details see www.velocebooks.com
email: info@veloce.co.uk • Tel: +44(0)1305 260068

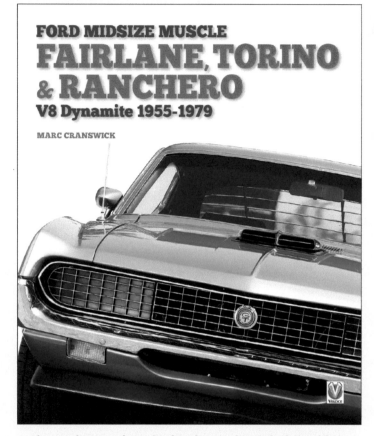

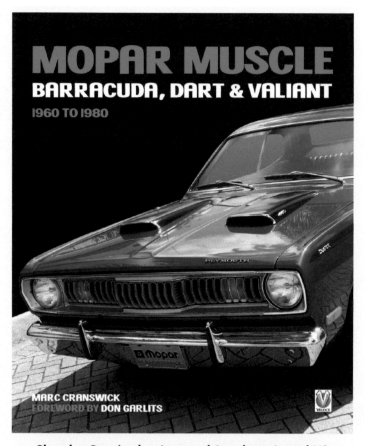

The evolution of Ford's family car through the golden era of Detroit. This book tells how Henry took the no-frills Fairlane, added more zing to create the Torino, and satisfied America's luxury desires with the LTD II; and follows the evolution of Ford's midsize muscle cars, to the creation of the first car-based pickup – the Ranchero.

ISBN: 978-1-845849-29-0
Hardback • 25x20.7cm • 176 pages • 229 pictures

Chrysler Corp's classic rear-drive slant six and V8 compacts of the '60s and '70s. From economy cars to muscle cars, from the street to the strip. The Mopar marvels that challenged rivals and inspired a generation.

ISBN: 978-1-787110-71-7
Hardback • 25x20.7cm • 176 pages • 290 colour and b&w pictures

www.velocebooks.com
shop • Veloce books • ebooks • apps • download our catalogue

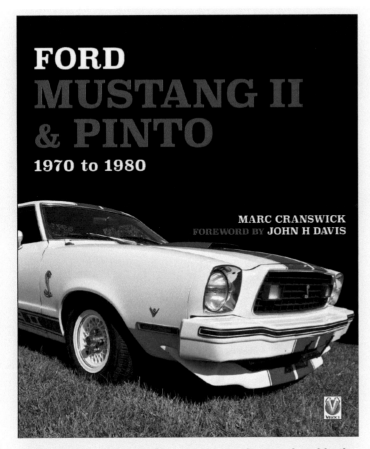

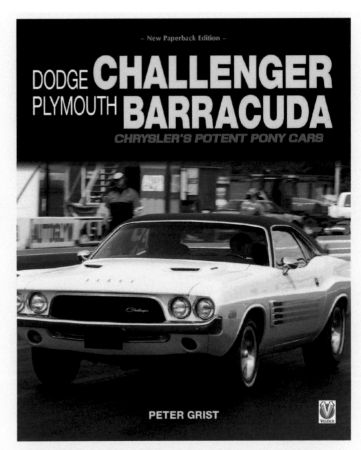

The history of Ford's first American-designed and built subcompacts. Following the Mustang II and Pinto through a challenging decade, as they competed with domestic and imported rivals in the showroom, and on the racetrack. This book examines icons of the custom car and racing scene, as Ford took Total Performance into a new era.

ISBN: 978-1-787112-67-4
Hardback • 25x20.7cm • 128 pages • 201 pictures

A Veloce Classic Reprint. In-depth look at the very desirable pony cars from Plymouth and Dodge that managed to beat the Ford Mustang to the dealerships, and went on to become one of the most sought-after classic car lines of all time.

ISBN: 978-1-787110-94-6
Paperback • 25x20.7cm • 192 pages • 375 pictures

For more information and price details, visit our website at www.velocebooks.com
email: info@veloce.co.uk • Tel: +44(0)1305 260068

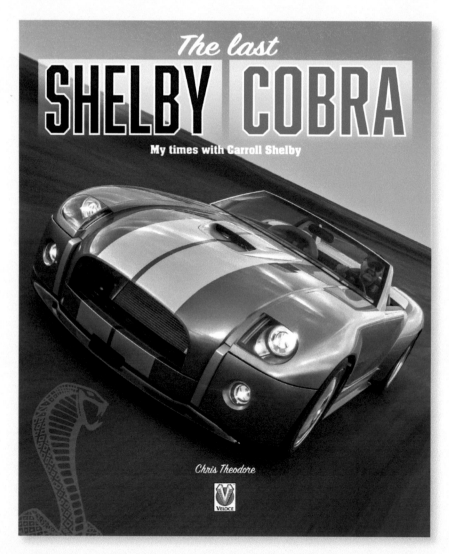

INDEX